COMMUNISM, CHRISTIANITY, DEMOCRACY

COMMUNISM, CHRISTIANITY, DEMOCRACY

Surjit Singh

 JOHN KNOX PRESS
Richmond, Virginia

For my Daughters,
Rita and Smita

Contents

Preface

Marxism-Leninism and liberal democracy are generalized world outlooks and compete with Christianity as a total view. The failure of Christianity in practice has historically given rise to these movements.

As secularized versions of Christianity they have tried to replace it in their respective spheres of influence. Christianity has been cut to size, but has managed to survive with a measure of vitality and a sense of penitence. The social condition of mankind offers it another opportunity to come alive and to become relevant to the personal and social needs of people.

The failure of the Marxist vision and the occurrence of the American social revolution provide two historic opportunities for the renewal of the life and mission of the church. In order to avail itself of these historic opportunities the church must unite and gather strength through the ecumenical process. Without being united the church will be inadequate for the task.

The whole discussion of the interrelations of communism, Christianity, and democracy occurs in the polarized and inwardly pluralized context of East and West, communism and democracy. The succeeding chapters unfold this story. Documentation would have required a different type of book, but indebtedness to the scholarship of others is evident on every page.

Surjit Singh

San Anselmo, California

1

Modern West and Russian East

> In the soul of the Russian people a struggle between East and West was waged, and that struggle is continuing in the Russian revolution. (Nicholas Berdyaev)

Soviet Russia is present and modern but its roots lie deep in the history of the imperial Russia of Peter, and the Russia of the Moscow, Tartar, and Kiev periods.

Russia's contact with the West starts in the fourteenth and fifteenth centuries when the Roman Catholic populations of Poland and Lithuania extended their domain on white Russian and Ukrainian people. This rule was solidified by two political and ecclesiastical events: the political union between Poland and Lithuania which took place in A.D. 1569, and the ecclesiastical union in A.D. 1594-96 between a sizable part of the Russian Orthodox Christian Community and the Roman Catholic Church. Western culture in its Polish assimilation and Western Christianity in its Roman Catholic Jesuit missionary enterprise were the two effective westernizing agents. Many members of the Russian Orthodox nobility went all the way to embrace Roman Catholicism rather than to remain members in a Uniate Church.

When these aggressive moves were taking place on the western approaches to Moscow, a counter pull was created in the East by the capture of Constantinople by the Ottoman Turks in A.D. 1453. Thus the mantle of Constantinople, "the second Rome," fell on

Moscow, "the third Rome." But the Muscovite Grand Duke was in
no position to fight on two fronts. In order to claim the East
Roman imperial heritage, he would have to fight the Osmanlis.
Military engagement with the Turks would have jeopardized the
desperate effort to save white Russia and the Ukraine from falling
into Western hands.

Between the fall of the "second Rome" on the one hand and
the Western trespass on the physical and spiritual soil of Russia on
the other, the broad stage was set for the unfolding of Russian
destiny in time and space, and for Russia's manifold encounters
with the whole Western world. This is the spectacle which we have
been beholding since the fifteenth century, and the end is not yet in
sight.

One of the early significant events was the retaking of Kiev
from Polish control in A.D. 1667. Kiev, the Ukrainian city which
had been the cultural and political center of pre-Muscovite Russia,
was a powerful station for transmitting Western ecclesiastical and
cultural influences into Russia. Although Polish Western forms
were weak and diluted, their influence on the Russian Orthodox
clergy was such that Peter the Great used them to good effect to
bring the Muscovite Orthodox Church in line with his westernizing
policy.

BYZANTIUM AND RUSSIA

From Byzantium to Russia came not only Christianity but also
a whole world view mixed with pagan occult and apocryphal elements.

The Christian world view made deep inroads into the Russian
soul, but it has been a puzzle why this did not result in productive
and creative thought. Reflecting on this phenomenon, the nineteenth-century Russian philosopher Chaadyaev has remarked that
Russia was untouched by the universal education of the human
race and that the Russians had not to date contributed any idea
which furthered the progress of human reason. The negative judgment of Chaadyaev and others may be due to a false comparison
between the growth of Russian culture from the thirteenth to the
seventeenth century, and that of west European culture during the
same period, the point being that the tempo and quality of west

European growth is considered normative and Russia is judged by this norm.

Rome was the radiating center for the spreading of Christianity to western Europe. Latin was a common language and there were no serious barriers. Latin also provided the contact with antiquity and thereby gave Europe a sense of rootedness. To Russia Christianity came from a distant and different land. Ecclesiastically Russia was indebted to Byzantium, but politically Russia was independent of Byzantium and lived in a world of her own.

Quite early the Russian Church began to free itself from the apron-strings of the Greek Church, and after the fall of Constantinople this movement gained momentum—so much so that Ivan IV told the Papal Legate: "Our faith is Christian and not Greek." Unlike Latin, Greek never became the language of church worship or of cultural communication. This linguistic isolation plus a distrustful attitude toward Western influences accounted in large measure for the cultural backwardness of Russia. It is little wonder that when channels of communications opened toward the West, many Russians became blind followers.

The influence of Byzantium on Russia has been profound and lasting, but one wonders why, in the wake of the fall of Constantinople, the Greek cultural leaders fled to the West and not to Russia. Perhaps the flowering of Russian Orthodox culture would have been early and significant if this migration had been diverted.

The first creative flowering showed itself in icon-painting. The great creations of Rublev in the late fourteenth and early fifteenth centuries, although still in the tradition of Byzantine icon-painting, is indicative of the awakening of Russian creative energies. It is sometimes said that the influence of Byzantine culture has been inhibitive on the Russian soul, but there is no evidence of Russian hostility to Byzantine culture. It is quite possible that linguistic isolation, lack of access to antiquity, and the suspicion of the West in its efforts to bring Russian Orthodox Christendom under the tutelage of Rome caused a deep crisis in the Russian consciousness. The Schism, in part, provided a creative channel for the liberation of the pent-up and restless energies in the Russian ecclesiastical and cultural consciousness.

MOSCOW, THE THIRD ROME

In the writings of a monk, Philotheus, appears the doctrine of Moscow as the third Rome. Writing at the end of the fifteenth century, he proclaims that the first and the second (Constantinople) Romes have fallen before the barbarians because of their heresies. Their place as the capital of the Christian world is now filled by Moscow. He also expressed the conviction that there never shall be a fourth Rome.

In Byzantium there already had developed the idea of a single emperor for the whole Christian world. The patriarch of Constantinople wrote to the Grand Prince Vasili I of Moscow when the latter refused to pay homage to the Byzantine emperor, saying that church and empire exist in a union and that it was impossible for Christians to have a church and not an emperor. Behind this kind of philosophy of history lies the prophecy of Daniel about the four kingdoms. After the fall of Constantinople the Russian thinkers were convinced that Providence had appointed Moscow, the third Rome, as the guardian of the purity of the church. The truth of Christ had been entrusted to the "chosen people" of Russian Orthodox Christendom. And since there was not to be a fourth Rome, the Russian Empire would last to the end of time.

THE SCHISM (RASKOL)

The Schism is interpreted generally as a problem of church ritual. It has, however, a deeper significance as the problem of empire and the ecclesiastical kingdom. Nikon, Archbishop of Novgorod, was made patriarch in 1652. He elicited a pledge of support from Czar Aleksei that the patriarch as the head of the church was above questioning in matters of interpretation regarding church rules and dogma. Among other things he introduced the three-fingered crossing and the threefold alleluia. This was against the accepted usage and was based upon the unpopular Greek service books. Moreover, Nikon was supported in these revisions by the Ukrainian scholars from Kiev, who were suspected by the Muscovites of having close connections with the Polish Catholics. The introduction of these changes was regarded as a weakening of the church, a prelude to the coming of the antichrist. Nikon moved swiftly to crush opposition and the reaction of the "Old Believers" was strong. They remained stubborn and unyielding in spite of suffering.

After Nikon declined in power, the Orthodox Church brought the state power in to crush the "Old Believers." The troops killed and imprisoned many. Others fled and yet quite a few of the "Old Believers" burned themselves alive rather than be taken in by government forces. Orthodoxy triumphed temporarily but the church was weakened internally and in its relation to the Czar.

On the deeper side, the Schism enshrined a philosophy of history. The ideal was the third Rome, the pure ecclesiastical kingdom. The church had a world mission of preserving the purity of Orthodox truth. The Old Believers considered themselves to be pure instruments of this world mission. Their problem was the antichrist, the secularization of the holy kingdom. They would sacrifice anything to prevent this. The utopian impasse is clear because the Old Believers regarded earthly Russia and Holy Russia as one and the same. Orthodoxy was more realistic. But in all this, Russian people and Orthodoxy paid dearly in men, talent, and resources, as is quite evident from the tragic history of Old Believers.

THE AGE OF PETER THE GREAT

Peter was a towering man of immense physical and mental energy. He set himself to the task of opening up Russia to manners and modes, ideas and techniques of the West. He became a frequent visitor to the German colony in Moscow and enjoyed himself to the limit in carousing and exchanging ideas with all sorts of people. He even took up smoking, much to the displeasure of the boyars—the bearded Russian nobility.

As a firm indication of his new style of doing things he built himself a new capital on the Gulf of Finland and called it St. Petersburg, after his own name. The new capital was a European city in contrast to the old semi-oriental Moscow. The shift from Moscow to St. Petersburg marked the opening of a new page in Russian history.

Peter was the first czar to go abroad. He headed an embassy

and traveled extensively in Europe. He loved to work with his hands. In order to learn naval science firsthand, he worked in disguise in a Dutch shipyard, where he also engaged in an internationally famous fistfight with a fellow worker. Everything in which the West excelled excited the imagination of the czar. He bought ships or had them built. He imported guns, machines, techniques, and technicians. He wanted to modernize and westernize Russia, and he performed his reforming task with such barbarity that the Old Believers labeled him antichrist.

There is, however, another interpretation of the age of Peter the Great. When Alexander Herzen was asked how Russia responded to the reforms of Peter, he answered that Russia responded by giving birth to Pushkin. Russia did not have anything comparable to the Reformation and the Renaissance. There are no Russian counterparts to Thomas Aquinas, Luther, Newton, or Voltaire. Compared to the West there is a cultural lag of many centuries. As a matter of fact it is wrong to compare Russia with the West in this manner. The innovations, pressures, and sufferings of the Petrine age bore fruit in the nineteenth century. Culturally speaking, the nineteenth century is the most creative and productive period in Russian history.

With a tremendous burst of energy Russia tried to close the cultural gap between herself and the West. As already noted in relation to icon-painting there were a few pioneers of art and thought, and M. V. Lomonosov was one who, in the eighteenth century, helped establish the Russian literary language. Some have ventured the judgment that if everything written in Russian (with few exceptions) till 1800 was destroyed the loss would be felt only by some specialized students. The ravages of the Tartar hordes, the censorious autocracy of the czars, the lethargic conservatism of the Orthodox Church, the constant drain of Russian energy through perpetual wars, and the conspicuous absence of great cities all conspired to arrest the cultural growth of Russia.

The nineteenth century gains real stature and importance against this background. The poets Pushkin and Lermontov; the novelists Tolstoy, Dostoevsky, Turgenev, and Gogol; the composers Tschaikovsky, Moussorgsky, Rimsky-Korsakov, Rubinstein, Borodin, and Glinka; the scientists Metchnikov, Mendeleev, and Pavlov; the historians Karamzin and Klyuchevsky; and artists such as Repin and Ivanov are the outstanding names (not to mention many lesser ones) that studded the Russian cultural firmament like bright luminaries. This does not mean that we are talking about individual men of genius, but rather that a Russian intelligentsia came into existence. It was small against the background of a large illiterate population, but in quality it was comparable to that in European countries.

TOLSTOY AND DOSTOEVSKY

Alexander Herzen called this period, particularly the reign of Czar Nicholas, one of outward slavery and inward liberation. This not only proved prophetic for what followed, but may also have lessons for the unfolding of contemporary Soviet history. Nicholas Berdyaev maintains that the inner revolution is best portrayed in the writings of Tolstoy and Dostoevsky, particularly the latter. Dostoevsky's novels are tragedies. His subject is man as historical and temporal being. He looks to the future for the freedom of the human spirit. This freedom will be religious freedom and will come with Christ and God.

Tolstoy wrote epics, and his novels are perfect because he dealt with man not in the setting of history but in the setting of the cosmos. He did not know Christ but only the teachings of Christ. In his own person Tolstoy was a revolutionary. He depicted the stricken conscience of nobility in relation to the poor masses. He was an equalitarian who believed in revolution without violence. He loved freedom to the point of being an anarchist. Both men were revolutionaries of the spirit and therefore were forerunners of the impending revolution. Both would have been equally horrified to learn that the Communist revolution resulted in the denial of the spirit.

SLAVOPHILISM AND WESTERNISM

Another reaction to the reforms of Peter was the construction of a philosophy of history in which the main problem under discussion was whether Russia is East or West. It is out of these deliberations that the two ways of viewing Russian history were born. Ivan Kireevsky is regarded as the founder of Russian Slavophilism. He came from a well-to-do family. He studied abroad and came under the influence of Hegel and Schelling. His Western orientation was considerably modified by his wife and he accepted a romantic view of the vast achievement and present mission of Russia.

Europe and Russia were different because they had different religions. Russia was the land of faith and divine truth because she was founded upon Eastern Orthodoxy. Believing in the doctrine of Moscow as the third Rome, Kireevsky taught that Russia was the custodian of true Christianity and therefore of true civilization. The West had diluted and lost the true faith because of the heresies of Roman Catholicism and Protestantism and the consequent religious warfare. It was, therefore, the mission of Russia to restore true Christianity to the West and to build a new civilization compounded of Russian and Western elements.

The distinguished theologian Khomyakov was the contemporary of Kireevsky and an ardent champion of Russian Orthodoxy against Roman Catholicism and Protestantism. Whereas Khomyakov was more nationalistic than Kireevsky, he nevertheless exposed the historical sins committed by Russia during and before the time of Peter. Constantine and Ivan Aksakov were brothers. Constantine maintained that Russia prior to Peter the Great was free from vices and that it was Peter who introduced these from the degenerated West. According to him Russia is both a country and a state. The country is an organic union of communities. But the state as coercive mechanism is necessary because of human shortcomings. To him the history of Russia is composed of the conflict between these two.

Ivan Aksakov connects Slavophilism with Pan-Slavism. He believes that the Russian Slavs have preserved the purity of Russian Orthodoxy and civilization. Roman Catholicism is the great enemy. It is, therefore, the duty of Russian Slavs to free their Slav brethren from the yoke of false religion and life and restore to them the true orthodox faith and civilization.

The main emphasis of the Slavophiles was that Russia and

Europe were distinct and had separate destinies. Russia, therefore, should not be forced to a European pattern. In support of their thesis they advocated an ideal of Orthodoxy based upon revelation and tradition. They exalted faith and emotion over reason and common sense and deferred to a benevolent but autocratic system of government. Men like Kireevsky had admitted the mistakes and shortcomings of Russia, but the later Slavophiles glossed over them. Whereas the earlier Slavophiles were idealistic about an Orthodoxy which never existed, the later ones made a simple equation between state and Orthodoxy. It is clear that there was a wide range of difference among the followers of Slavophilism, yet on the whole most of them favored abolition of serfdom, increase in personal liberty, and the curtailment of the powers of the bureaucracy. In this manner they had much in common with the Westerners and could not be simply described as conservative over against liberal.

Alexander Herzen, in describing the relation between Slavophiles and Westerners, says that they are like the two-faced Janus; one regarding Russia as mother and the other regarding her as child. In the 1830's and 1840's they met and debated in the same living rooms, as the well-known Aksakov and Belinsky exemplify. But later the distance grew between them, as is clearly indicated by Belinsky's refusal to meet his friend Aksakov.

The most sensitive, cultured, and thoughtful people in the nineteenth century did not live in the present. The Slavophiles transported themselves to the Russia before Peter the Great, and Westerners dreamed of an idealized West. However, there are some utopian elements common to both. According to Nicholas Berdyaev the most interesting type of Westerner was the one who made a rehash of the Germanic philosophy of Hegel and Schelling and the French socialism of Saint-Simon and Fourier. Here philosophic wholeness and social wholeness are fused together. This total outlook is a Russian characteristic and persists in Marxism-Leninism.

The greatest difference, and that upon which the Westerners laid the heaviest emphasis, was that Russia and western Europe were not different in kind but only degree; Russia was following the same kind of development and the main task ahead was to catch up with the West. In other words, the Westerners denied that

Russia and Russian religion and culture had any unique destiny. In addition, the Westerners were not oriented toward Orthodoxy but were rationalistic and agnostic, and one institution which they admired and wanted to establish in Russia was constitutional government.

The highly cultured and tragic figure of Chaadyaev is a lesson in itself. In his "Philosophical Letter" he delivered a judgment on the past history of Russia. According to him, Russia had no great achievement to its credit; it had shown no unique destiny and had not produced anything great. He was haunted by the thought that he was condemned to live in a backward country under despotic rule. He was considered dangerous by the czar. He was subjected to a medical examination and pronounced insane. In this way he was silenced and crushed. However, he wrote "A Madman's Apology" in which he affirmed the destiny of the Russian people based upon their latent powers. When these powers were awakened the Russians would perform their characteristic mission—a social mission. Here we have a philosophy of history, pessimistic about the past but hopeful about the future, with a thrust of social messianism.

Many cultural Russians sought their salvation by traveling the whole length of the journey to Roman Catholicism. Pecherin, who typifies this reaction, went abroad and became a Roman Catholic monk. He fused his utopian socialism with Roman Catholicism and fervently believed that Russia would open a new chapter in world history. Vissarion Belinsky is perhaps the greatest literary critic of Russia in the nineteenth century. He used the medium of literary criticism for the setting forth of his social and political ideas, which were largely of Western inspiration. He put his stock in reason and knowledge over against faith and revelation. In writing to Gogol, Belinsky asserted that the salvation of Russia lay in the advancement of civilization, education, and humanity, which would arouse the suppressed sense of dignity of the people. He felt that serfdom and bodily punishment should be abolished and the administration of justice should be strictly applied.

Belinsky traveled through the full gamut of ideas current in Russia during the 1840's. Philosophically he passed through the discipleship of Fichte, Schelling, and Hegel. His searchings later led him to Feuerbach. This is quite significant in relation to Marxian development in Russia. From the point of social philosophy he absorbed the influence of French literature and social thought. As a literary critic he was the first to appreciate the literary creations of Pushkin, Gogol, and earlier creative writers. Belinsky struggled manfully to achieve an integrated outlook which would combine the theoretical and the practical and would provide answers to all the questions of life. Because of censorship, the only way social and human concerns could be expressed was through literary criticism. In Belinsky the crisis of Hegelianism expressed itself in the affirmation of living human personality. This conflict was further resolved into a desperate search for a social structure of society. In this way individualistic socialism was formulated in Russia.

According to Berdyaev, Belinsky was deeply disillusioned by idealism. He became a revolutionary socialist. But the significant fact is that through him revolutionary socialism was aligned with atheism. The basis of his atheism was profound sympathy with humanity and the inability to relate excessive suffering in life with the idea of God. Here we see a movement in Russian thought comparable to that which occurred in Germany in the left-wing Hegelianism of Feuerbach and Marx. In the name of sympathy for humanity, Belinsky turned to the preaching of tyranny and brutality, and can be called the forerunner of Bolshevik morals.

Outwardly and inwardly, technologically and ideologically, the interaction between Russia and the West spans the period of three hundred years. Whereas the ideological interaction will be discussed later in depth, the present discussion can be concluded by showing the impact of the technological interaction.

Arnold Toynbee maintains that the response of Russia to the Polish military occupation of Moscow in A.D. 1610-12 was the revolution of Peter the Great, which not only defeated the Poles and extended the Russian frontier, but ultimately vindicated itself by defeating Napoleon, the greatest European soldier of the day, in A.D. 1812. But Western military technique stole a march over Russia, as is witnessed by the American Civil War and Bismarckian Prussia's Wars. For herself, Russia found out in 1905

against Japan and more disastrously in 1914-18 at the hands of
Germany that Petrine arms and techniques were a poor match for
advanced technology. Once again she was determined to catch up
with the West. Russia responded by becoming Communist and
mastering Western military techniques. The Soviet Union proved
herself the equal of the West by Stalin's victory over Hitler in
1945. But no sooner could the Soviet Union consolidate its war
gains than the Americans exploded the atom bomb and later the
hydrogen bomb. The Russian Communists responded by their
atom and hydrogen bombs, and in launching the Sputnik in 1957
stole a march over the West in that category of military technology.

The arms race with its seesaw character seems to have come to
rest for the time being in the limited-test-ban treaty of 1962. The
partial nuclear freeze opens up many other avenues and possibilities of East-West interaction. There is both risk and promise for
civilization and the life of man in the post-limited-test-ban period.

2

Christianity in Russia and the Soviet Union

Christianity came into Russia about the middle of the tenth century in the form of Eastern Orthodoxy. The Varangians who had served under the emperors of Constantinople brought it to Russia, and Olga, wife of the Varangian Prince Igor of Kiev, adopted it as her own religion. It was, however, her grandson Vladimir who urged the men of Russia to accept the religion of the Greeks of Constantinople.

By the end of the tenth century there appeared two forms of the relationship between church and state. In the West the Roman Catholic churchman Hildebrand, later Pope Gregory VII, forcefully propounded the doctrine that the pope, being the lineal descendant of Peter, had complete and final jurisdiction over Christendom. Gregory maintained that the pope could depose rulers and absolve their subjects from allegiance to them. He actually rebuked the kings of France and Spain and in 1077 forced the proud Holy Roman Emperor to come to Canossa.

In the East, however, the position of the patriarch of Constantinople was quite the reverse. He had to follow the pattern set by Constantine who convened and presided over the Council of Nicea and arrested and imprisoned Arius and his followers. Succeeding emperors followed the same rule. They deposed patriarchs at will and regarded themselves, in the terms of Leo III, as emperors and priests. In Russia, Peter the Great is the example of this type of

relation between church and state. In the ninth century Emperor
Basil, the Macedonian, advocated the theory of "symphony" or
harmonious equality of emperor and patriarch. This remained only
a theory. In practice the prior theory prevailed. The patriarchs,
even the most powerful among them, never attained equality with
the emperor.

This is the church the Russians inherited. It was rich in sym-
bolism and ornate in ritual, but always subservient to the civil
power. If the Western form of the church-state relation was
called "Papocaesarism," then this was "Caesaropapism."

The Mongol invasion shattered the political structure of Russia, but the church managed to keep in one piece the fabric of
Russian society. The passing of the Mongol threat and the sacking
of Constantinople by the Turks convinced the Russians of the
moral bankruptcy of the Greeks and assured them of their own
strength and destiny. In 1547 Ivan the Terrible became czar and
declared himself emperor and priest. His son Feodor, assisted by
Boris Godunov, chose the first Russian patriarch. Now Russian
state and church were free from Byzantium. Peter the Great let the
patriarchate lapse and instituted in its place a corporate body
called "The Most Holy Synod." The members of the Synod were
obliged to take the following oath: "I recognize and confirm with
my oath that the supreme judge of this Holy Synod is the Emperor
of all the Russias." The oath makes sure that no conflict will arise
against the interests of the state. The church was now subordinated
to the state more than ever before.

In the nineteenth century this subordination became even more
acute. In 1817 Czar Alexander I created a ministry of Religious
Affairs and Public Education. The Synod and all other non-
Orthodox denominations were placed under it. The church lost
whatever little freedom it had before. But when in 1824 this ministry was abolished, the over-procurator, also called "the eye of
the czar," became all the more powerful. He made sure that the
bishops were politically reliable.

From this brief glimpse of the history of the Russian Church
we learn that the pattern of the church-state relationship was set
in Byzantium. The pattern did not deviate in any significant way

till the beginning of the twentieth century. It now remains to be seen what shape it assumed under Bolshevik rule in the Soviet Union.

CHRISTIANITY IN THE SOVIET UNION

The Soviet regime from its inception recognized the importance of the Orthodox Church. It was the church in power in Petrograd and Moscow. It was not, however, quite the same church which served the last of the Romanov czars. Two days before the Bolshevik take-over, a Russian Church council elected Tikhon as patriarch. This was significant because none had been elected since 1721, when Peter the Great abolished the patriarchal office. Under Tikhon's leadership the church supported the counterrevolution. The church fought the Communist regime and declared it anathema.

This interference of the church in politics led the government to pay special attention to its activities. The church suffered as a result of the political activities of priests who supported the extreme rightist organizations. The government at first could not assess the full significance of the church, but later came to regard it as a cultural expression of the continuity of the Russian people.

The Soviet Government passed a decree in 1918 declaring full legal equality of all religious groups, thereby disestablishing the Russian Orthodox Church. In spite of this action the Orthodox Church continued to enjoy pre-eminence among religious denominations because of its history and numerical strength. Moreover, the Government needed it on the world religious front, and this involved special deference to it. It was a kind of seesaw relationship between the church and the state, the state once persecuting the church and another time tolerating it. The Government passed a decree in 1922 requiring the churches to surrender their treasures and other valuables for famine relief. Under the direction of Patriarch Tikhon, bishops and priests resisted the surrender of church treasures. The Government by its power and tactics put the church in a position where it appeared to be defending church property over against the poor plight of the famine-stricken people. It not only tended to alienate the people but brought down heavy persecution upon the church.

It had the further effect of causing division in the church itself. Some bishops and priests refused to follow the lead of the patriarch. The Soviet Government was now in a position to play off one section of the church against the other. Bishops and priests testified against other bishops and priests who had taken their stand against parting with church treasures and property. The division undermined the cohesion of the church and forced Patriarch Tikhon to surrender his office to another.

Many schismatic church parties came into existence. Some characterized themselves as the "Living Church," and a "Union of Church Regeneration," while others called themselves "Union of Parishes of the Ancient Apostolic Church" and "Russian People's Church." They all fitted in the general pattern of reform movement. They formed themselves into a coalition under the general name of "Supreme Church Administration." Compared to the patriarchal church, they were subservient to the Soviet regime and openly in favor of communism. They embodied their political views in an "Address to the Government." The address asserted that the Soviet Government was fighting for the ideals of the Kingdom of God and that every member of the church should be loyal to the political power and help it against the evil in the world.

The people who joined the reform movement were called "Renovators." They were in favor of a progressive church clearly disassociated from the czarist tradition. The renovating priests conducted worship in Russian rather than in church Slavonic, and celebrated the eucharist in full view of the congregation rather than being screened behind the altar. The "Renovators" also demanded that married priests should be made bishops and went ahead to consecrate their bishops irrespective of canon law.

The schism in the church was comforting to the Government. The Communist Party openly declared that this division should be fully exploited to the total downfall of the enemy. The Communists regarded the old church as belonging to the upper classes and the new church as belonging to the petty bourgeoisie. Conflict was, therefore, inevitable from both sides of the church.

The "Renovators" by being pro-Government did not really win the confidence of the Communists, although the Government granted them a measure of privilege within limits. They were permitted to issue a periodical and to have their priests trained in Moscow and Leningrad, and until 1927 they were the only officially recognized Orthodox Church body. Moreover they were indirectly strengthened by the government action which deported the bishops who had been loyal to the Patriarch Tikhon.

It looked for a time as if this new church had come to stay, but this also turned out to be an episode in Russian church history. The majority of Orthodox laymen viewed the Renovators with suspicion, and it was their hostility that caused the failure of this movement. Also by this time the old church had gradually changed its attitude toward the Government, and having accepted the fact of Soviet rule, became loyal to it.

The telling example of this change of position was Patriarch Tikhon's statement in which he promised that he would no longer be an enemy of the Government. He disassociated himself from monarchists and counterrevolutionaries and in a second statement he offered his apologies for his past anti-Soviet actions. In return the Government released him from custody and never brought him to trial. However, Tikhon died before he could do anything effective to heal the schism, and after his death, a scramble for ecclesiastical power caused further division in the church.

Metropolitan Peter Polyansky remained a nominal head, whereas Metropolitan Sergius Starogorodsky emerged as victor in the struggle for power, but only in 1927 was able to administer effectively. That year he made a statement identifying himself with the Soviet Union. The statement, ratified by the newly convened Holy Synod, declared that the joys and successes of the Soviet State were the joys and successes of the church. This was not only the affirmation of what Tikhon had said, but much more. It was a full profession of political patriotism. Any action of war, boycott, or murder aimed at the Soviet State was equally directed against the church. It could be that the vigorous nature of the statement was in part attributable to the murder of Voikov, the Russian ambassador to Warsaw, by a nineteen-year-old Russian emigré.

The emigré was a devoted member of the church and had witnessed the Revolution as a little boy. He had been a server in the
church at Samara, which the Communists had converted into a
dancing hall. This he could not forget, and avenged it by the
murder. The church was put on the spot indirectly by a misguided
action.

The statement of Sergius brought government recognition for
his ecclesiastical administration and permission to publish the
Journal of the Moscow Patriarchate. But there was no peace in the
church. There were those who did not approve of collaboration
with the state and chose the path of martyrdom, repudiating Sergius' statement of 1927. Moreover, the Communists, sensing that
perhaps the people thought religion was all right, stepped up their
antireligious action and atheistic propaganda. The antireligious
agitators between 1929 and 1932 carried on a merciless campaign
for closing of churches and confiscation of church bells.

The League of Militant Godless attacked religious beliefs in
general, but indulged in particular in personal attacks upon individual priests. Ever since Sergius made the statement that the interests
of the state and church were identical, the parish priests in the
countryside felt the crushing hand of the authorities who were bent
upon exterminating religion in very much the same way as they
liquidated private agriculture by collectivizing it.

Priests were held as hostages and were arrested and shot if
they or their parishioners obstructed political authority. They were
considered second-rate citizens. Until the Stalin Constitution in
1936, the priests were denied the right to vote. They were labeled
as exploiters and could not join trade unions or get ration cards for
food. They could not get any gainful employment, and in Byelo-
russia they were even forbidden to be peasants. In view of the
official terror many priests had broken relation with the church,
but even by this action they did not merit the confidence of the
state. The children of priests were not accepted into institutions of
higher learning. The voting rights of priests were restored only
after they had performed five years of socially useful and productive work in loyalty to the state. To become a full citizen again was
a long and arduous affair. Even the 1936 Constitution did not, in

fact, change their real status. Although they were given voting rights, in the estimation of Communists they remained exploiters of the peasants. The Constitution gave them the equality of citizenship, but when they applied for a job in a school they were told that as members of a cult they could not become teachers.

During 1937 the NKVD (secret police) came up with the discovery and evidence of a string of plots against the state. A case had even been prepared against Metropolitan Sergius who among other things was accused of sending a message to the Japanese intelligence. The message was in fact a simple fraternal greeting to his namesake in Japan. The NKVD evidently could not lay its hands on Sergius without the explicit permission of Stalin, and Stalin had evidently decided against it. Stalin was wise in his decision, because the unfolding of historical events showed that he needed the help of the metropolitan. Sergius had been co-operating with the Government since 1927. But this co-operation was from a position of weakness.

Only after 1939, when the Soviet regime annexed territories with Orthodox Christian populations, was the church in a position to negotiate from some kind of strength. The state needed the church to absorb these people into the Soviet sphere of influence. However, a much more drastic change in church-state relations occurred in 1941 when Nazis invaded Russia. The church became cofighter with the state against Hitler's aggression, and was able to overcome its earlier humiliating role.

The loyalty and steadfastness of millions of Russians to their church impressed the regime and gradually led to the acceptance of the church as a fact of Russian existence. Moreover, Hitler did not single out communism as a target for attack, but invaded Russia as a people and a nation. This made the national interest more prominent. The Communist regime began to look at the Russian Orthodox Church in a historical and nationalistic way. This was reciprocated by the church. Hence a new opportunity arose by which a concordat could be established between church and state.

The party-line Communists interpreted the return to Orthodoxy as weakmindedness. But this could hardly help their idealogy if people in the time of need and emergency turned to the church rather than to them. In the hours of peril even the Communists could not afford to indulge in antireligious propaganda. Their main concern was to enlist the support of millions of Orthodox believers for the successful conclusion of the war. The church and state fought side by side to save the Russian nation, its historical heritage, and its present government. A new and nationalistic evaluation of Russian history entered into Communist considerations. They began to take pride in Slav brotherhood and even in saints of the Orthodox Church such as Dimitry Donskoy and Alexander Nevsky who were also statesmen and military commanders.

Metropolitan Shimansky remained in Leningrad throughout the siege of the city, and Metropolitans Sergius and Nikolay spent the worst years of the war in Moscow. The faithful of the church made material sacrifices for the war effort. They provided a fighter squadron named "Alexander Nevsky" for the air force and presented a tank column called "Dimitry Donskoy" for the army. Sergius issued twenty-three proclamations to the faithful to fight the pagan hordes of Hitler in the name of Christianity as well as of Russia. In 1942 Metropolitan Nikolay was appointed a member of the Extraordinary State Commission of Inquiry to look into the crimes committed on Soviet territory by German fascists and their collaborators. This was very significant because it brought about a working alliance between the Communist Party, the patriotic church, and nonparty figures.

The Soviet Government accorded recognition to the patriotic co-operation and loyalty of the church. On September 4, 1943, Marshal Stalin received Metropolitans Sergius, Alexis, and Nikolay in the Kremlin. This was a memorable event, and the subsequent history of the Russian Orthodox Church is directly traceable to it. An understanding was evidently reached by which the church came to know what to expect from the Government. The concessions which the church received are quite remarkable.

The church was permitted to elect its patriarch and to re-establish ecclesiastical government. It elected Sergius as patriarch and reconstituted the Holy Synod. All this was expedited in a matter of a few days. The church council which approved these actions was quite small: it consisted of nineteen people. It is reported that a large number of church leaders were either in prisons or concentration camps. The *Journal of the Moscow Patriarchate* started publication again after having been suspended in 1936. Permission was granted to open theological seminaries and the church was declared a "judicial person" entitled to hold and administer property. This recognition was granted to all religious bodies and not only to the Orthodox Church. The Soviet State recognized the Russian Orthodox Church as the principal religious body in the land, and as the sole representative of the Orthodox Christians in the U.S.S.R. Only the Orthodox Church of Georgia was exempted from this rule. This dealt a death blow to the earlier prevailing idea of the equality of different religious bodies.

The "Renovators" or the "Living Church" to which the Soviet regime had been partial earlier also had to fall in line with the new concordat. Once Sergius was made the patriarch, the leaders of the schismatic church made their humble submission to him and reverted to the status which they had held prior to the schism. As a practical consequence the churches of the Renovators with all their properties reverted to the old church. It is difficult to say if this conversion of the schismatics was voluntary. The Soviet regime had no interest in maintaining the "Living Church" the moment it was realized that its strength was fractional over against the old church. It was the war effort which made this fact patently obvious.

As a formal recognition of the patriarch's church, the Government created a special "Council for the Affairs of the Russian Orthodox Church." The chairman of the council was nicknamed "People's Commissar for Opium." He has been regarded as the equivalent of the over-procurator, the eyes and the ears of the czars. There are, however, some differences. Under the czars the post was supposed to be held by a Christian believer, whereas under the Communists he must be a convinced atheist. The czars accorded the over-procurator a very high status; but it was difficult to assess the role and its importance under the Soviet power. It does not seem to be very significant. The establishment of the council has caused a return to prerevolutionary times when there was not the same kind of hostility which was present at the beginning of the Soviet regime.

The council's terms of reference are not precisely known. It acts as a liaison between the government and the patriarch. The patriarch cannot approach any state ministry directly. The council also has representatives in all the different republics. At least one representative is allocated to one diocesan bishop. The council has provided legal and material facilities for the opening of new churches and the restoration of old ones. It is also the council's duty to look after the needs and comforts of church dignitaries, particularly the patriarch. It is their task to see that the church dignitaries within an atheist state are treated with the same dignity as prelates of the Western churches. It is, however, the inevitable function of the council to see that church action and policy conform to the interest of the state. The council makes recommendations for promotion and elevation, and from its close observation it recommends which hierarchs can be sent abroad safely. In these functions there is considerable similarity between the office of the over-procurator and the council.

Sergius reigned as patriarch for only eight months. When he died on May 15, 1944, his functions were taken over by Metropolitan Alexis of Leningrad and Novgorod. He had been closely associated with the policies of Sergius and therefore it was natural for him to step into his place. In his very first statement he reaffirmed the loyalty of the church to the state. He assured Stalin that he would guide the church away from mistakes and miscalculations, and expressed his own deep affection and gratitude to him.

In the interim period before Alexis became patriarch, the war situation underwent a radical change. From a war to defend the homeland, it became a war of conquest. Russian troops were conquering part of Germany and occupying Hungary, Serbia, Bulgaria, and Romania by routing the Germans from there. There were Orthodox Christian populations in these countries. The church was called upon to act beyond Soviet frontiers to promote loyalty and friendship among the Balkan people toward the Soviet

Union. Also at home the church was of considerable assistance in enhancing the respectability of the regime among the Russian people. There were also a large number of "White Russian" emigrés living in the West. The Russian Orthodox Church could be used either to promote friendship among them toward the Soviet Union, or failing that, to cause confusion in their midst. Moreover, the church could be of great help in establishing the friendly liaison with the Orthodox patriarchates of the Orient in case the Soviet Union decided to cultivate intensive diplomatic relations with the Middle East.

It became quite clear that although the war had been won there was ample scope for the continuance of friendly church-state relations. As the Soviet Union became a great power, it was led by the logic of international relations to enhance the power and prestige of the Russian Orthodox Church as a great ecclesiastical world power. This may be part of the reason behind the pomp and show which accompanied the election of Patriarch Alexis in 1945 and the celebration of the five-hundredth anniversary of the autonomous Russian Orthodox Church in 1948. And all this took place in Moscow, the capital of an avowed atheist Communist state. One can note the contrast between the election of Sergius and that of Alexis. The first was modest and attended by only nineteen clerics. For the second, there were elaborate preparations, and the church council was attended by 204 church dignitaries and laymen. The patriarchs of Antioch and Alexandria were in attendance along with the distinguished representatives of the patriarchs of Constantinople, Bulgaria, Romania, and Serbia. The Soviet Government's representative, G. G. Karpov, praised the Russian Orthodox Church for its patriotic role in history and particularly for its loyalty and support in World War II. He also strongly hinted that the Soviet Government would be well pleased if the patriotic and respected churchman Alexis were to be elected as the patriarch. All this is an open demonstration that the relations between church and state had been much improved.

The 1945 church council greatly impressed the foreign visitors and the Russian Church. For such a religious demonstration to take place in the neighborhood of Moscow was a unique event in

itself. It brought to the Russian Orthodox Church the reminis-
cences and the hope of Moscow as the third Rome. Metropolitan
Benjamin gave expression to these messianic ideas when he said
that Moscow might become the third Rome and in the future the
whole church would gather there. In his opinion, Moscow could
become the seat of an advisory council linking all the Orthodox
Churches around the world.

The Soviet authorities responded sympathetically to the idea of
Moscow's becoming a world ecclesiastical center. Patriarch Alexis
was encouraged to seek foreign contacts and to enhance the importance of his church in the world. As a matter of fact, Generalis-
simo Stalin himself assured Alexis and Metropolitan Nikolay of his
support in 1945 at a follow-up meeting of 1943. Matters such as
the training of priests, the publication of religious literature, and
the proposed tour of the patriarch to the Middle East were discussed. Molotov, who was first Deputy Premier and Foreign Minis-
ter, attended the meeting and was entrusted with making the tour
of the patriarch as smooth and successful as possible. It is rare that
such a deluxe treatment is accorded by non-Communist governments to their church dignitaries. An aircraft piloted by a hero of
the Soviet Union was put at the disposal of the patriarch.

The patriarch's visit to the Middle East lasted four weeks and
bore much fruit. It brought the Russian Orthodox Church closer to
the Orthodox churches in the area. It was able to reclaim properties that belonged to the Russian Church prior to the October
Revolution. But above all the visit resulted in a very favorable
publicity for the Soviet Union with lasting good effects. The Soviet
forces were in occupation of central and southeastern Europe and
Manchuria. This opened up a vast area of operation for the church
under the protective wing of the Soviet state. The envoys of the
church were received with honor wherever they went. Scattered Orthodox groups and Russian emigrés affirmed their allegiance to the
church. Many of these groups turned to the church in the hope that
they and their families would be spared the punishment resulting
from collaboration with the Nazis and Japanese. The Orthodox
Church in Manchuria came around and swelled the ranks of the
Muscovite episcopate by one metropolitan, one archbishop and
two bishops. The Orthodox communities in China waited until the

Communist take-over and then declared their allegiance. Those in the Russian zones of Germany and Austria acted in the same manner. Even in countries where Moscow's political influence was not great there were favorable reactions. In France the Orthodox Church was affiliated with the patriarch of Constantinople, but in 1945 it acknowledged the Russian patriarch without breaking relations with the former.

In those countries where the local Orthodox churches thought their relation to Moscow would be detrimental to their interest, there was little or no success. In 1947 the metropolitan of Leningrad was sent to the United States to bring back into the fold the Russian Orthodox Church of North America. The church in America was ready to acknowledge the spiritual headship but not the legal jurisdiction of the patriarch of Moscow. Only about ten percent remained loyal to him. Patriarch Alexis visited Bulgaria and Romania and established the closest relationship with these countries. The Orthodox churches of Czechoslovakia and Poland were given autonomous status. The few Orthodox parishes in Hungary were put under the jurisdiction of Moscow.

In 1947 the patriarch of Moscow made a most daring attempt to call all the heads of the Orthodox churches for a conference in Moscow. He proposed that Russian, English, French, and Greek be the languages of the conference, and that the subject matter of discussions be the interrelationships of the Orthodox churches, the Vatican, and the ecumenical movement. This kind of ambitious program could not have been put forward without the support of the Soviet Government. The pan-Orthodox conference did not materialize because the patriarchs of Constantinople and Alexandria declined the invitation. The patriarch of Moscow did not give up the conference, but invited the heads of the churches to come for the celebration of the five-hundredth anniversary of canonical independence of the Russian Orthodox Church. The celebration was to precede the conference and the hope was that the conference could still be held. The heads of the churches sent their representatives, who returned home immediately after the celebrations. Mr. Karpov accused the nonattending heads of the churches of boycotting the conference for nonreligious reasons.

In the contest for world power the Kremlin launched a new

crusade for peace on an ambitious scale. The Russian Orthodox Church, and the other churches to a lesser extent, took a full part in this campaign for peace. The *Journal of the Moscow Patriarchate* devoted from one-third to one-half of its valuable space to the reproduction and publication of peace information. Since the *Journal* was the only publication of the church, this took away a lot of space for political purposes. This political space was badly needed for religious ends. The church had to reproduce in its *Journal* what had already appeared in the secular press. The Soviet Government re-established the so-called wartime common front among the Communists, the church, and nonparty people. The alliance at this time was more formally organized. In the context of church-state relations this was a new opportunity for the church to secure its place by showing its usefulness to the state. The state on the other hand recognized the church as an important social factor. The church also lent the peace movement a respectability which it might not have enjoyed otherwise.

The church, the Communists, and the nonparty people worked together for political purposes through organizations such as the "Soviet Peace Defense Committee" and the "All Union Conferences for the Defense of Peace." The church was very strongly represented in these conferences. The delegations of the church consisted of the patriarch, metropolitans, archbishops, bishops, and priests. Metropolitan Nikolay was usually the church spokesman at such conferences. He also represented the church on the "Soviet Peace Committee" which was composed of 110 representatives from different walks of life in the nation. Metropolitan Nikolay received much publicity for his speeches and peace activities. Even the schoolchildren were puzzled because they had been taught the harmfulness of religious teachings. The ordinary Soviet citizen was also confused about these activities of the church. The church appeared to the public as the ardent champion of peace on earth, and under the limiting circumstances of the day it is difficult to conceive how the church could assume an ideal posture of its own.

The peace statements of the Russian Orthodox Church and the speeches of Nikolay were mixed with political passion. They were anti-Western. The political passion of Nikolay was not that of a

Communist fellow traveler, but of a nationalist who looked at the Soviet Union as a new expression of eternal Russia. In his speeches he seemed to prefer words such as "homeland" or "fatherland" instead of "the Soviet Union." It would be untrue to say that the church did not try to give religious meaning to the peace campaign. When Patriarch Alexis exhorted the clergy to sign the Stockholm Peace Appeal, he said that they would be doing so in obedience to Christ's commandment of love. Metropolitan Nikolay said that God is the source of peace, and that Christians should dedicate themselves with all their strength to the task of achieving peace. The Russian Orthodox Church was quite parochial in its judgments on the wider Western world. The factual basis of its judgments was derived from the information based on the censored sources of Soviet Government. Much of the emotional content of the anti-Western and anti-Roman Catholic statements can be attributed to a lack of objective knowledge about the outside world.

AFTER STALIN

Peace propaganda after the death of Stalin became more subtle and sensitive and hence more palatable from the viewpoint of the church. The death of Stalin affected all aspects of Soviet life, including the church. The church had been equally ardent about the Stalin cult, and just as Stalin was praised in Communist gatherings, so was he eulogized by patriarch, bishop, and priest from the pulpits of great cathedrals. The church even called him the defender of the faith. This must have sounded extraordinarily odd to Communist ears. But if one keeps in mind the historical relationship between Orthodoxy and the czars, then this may not sound so strange after all. The church knew that Stalin could have ruined her, but largely for reasons of state he did not attempt anything of that sort. In gratitude, the whole episcopate sent him a collective letter on his seventieth birthday. The patriarch sent a most effusive letter to the Council of Ministers at the death of Stalin. In the letter, the patriarch acknowledged with deep appreciation Stalin's benevolent attitude toward the needs of the church and vouched for the everlasting enshrinement of his memory in the heart of the church. Church dignitaries provided a guard of honor when his body was lying in state. The patriarch received messages of condolence from church leaders around the world. All this was done in accordance with the concordat established between church and state. But the death of Stalin must have also aroused second thoughts about the continuance of the concordat.

A collective leadership took charge after Stalin. The problems of take-over were so overwhelming that during this period the church and the opponents of the church were left relatively alone. Although the chances of antireligious activity grew, the church relaxed a little bit from the harassment of the secret police. The church was also able to have more foreign contacts. But the return of Communist policy to Lenin and Leninism opened grave possibilities for the repudiation of the concordat and was an open encouragement to the atheistic propagandists to launch attacks aimed at the church. In the middle of 1954 all the press organs of the Soviet Union suddenly turned violently against the church. *Pravda,* the official organ of the Communist Party, gave the first signal of attack. This must have had the blessings of high authority, for the barrage continued unabated for almost three months. Mr. Georgii Karpov, having heard complaints and countercomplaints, said that both citizen and clergy were to blame for what happened.

The Communist leadership was led to reaffirm the policy of concordat. There was rivalry and struggle for power in the highest place of Communist authority, and in order to win popular support, even of the church, they tried to outdo each other. Khrushchev, speaking for the central committee of the Communist Party, issued a decree entitled, "About mistakes in conducting scientific-atheistic propaganda among the population." The statement did not mean the stopping of antireligious propaganda. But because it acknowledged the loyal support of the church, it was interpreted as hands-off policy in relation to the Russian Orthodox Church in particular. Georgii Malenkov, who was the chairman of the Council of Ministers, did not want to trail behind his rival, and called into audience Patriarch Alexis. However, the days of Malenkov were just about over, and Bulganin soon succeeded him, continuing the politically expedient policy of making limited concessions to the church.

The new flexible foreign policy of coexistence opened up broad areas for the collaboration of church and state. Under Stalin's regime the church made pointed and hostile statements at the Vatican and the Roman Catholic Church. The *Journal of the Moscow Patriarchate* was conciliatory under the new policy and the Holy Synod showed keen interest in the ecumenical movement. The Russian Orthodox Church was permitted to have large-scale contacts with the Western church. Facilities of travel were provided for the cultivation of these contacts. The leaders of the Orthodox Church traveled to Britain, West Germany, and the U.S.A. Similarly, the leaders of the Western churches traveled to the Soviet Union. The visits of the Western leaders led to the study of conditions on the spot and was productive of better knowledge of churches and their leaders. It also tended to blunt the edge of criticism. Internally the church acquired a better bargaining position in relation to the Kremlin.

During the new policy of peaceful coexistence the foreign relations of the church and the foreign diplomacy of the Soviet Union became closely intertwined. This happened as a natural course of development; but it also was equally true that when political relations went sour with a particular country, the religious relations also terminated. For instance, when the Soviet Union and Yugoslavia fell out, no churchmen of either country exchanged visits. As a matter of fact, at the height of the conflict the patriarch condemned Yugoslavia for having joined the camp of the warmongers, and returned to it the Order of National Liberation conferred on him under happier circumstances. But once peace was made between Khrushchev and Tito, the Serbian patriarch visited the Soviet Union in 1956, and in 1957 the visit was returned by Patriarch Alexis. Episodes such as these go to show how free the church in the Soviet Union can expect to be—or, in fact, is!

The Soviet Union started a new custom in 1955. It began to invite the representatives of the Russian Orthodox Church to diplomatic receptions. It seems that when Bulganin and Khrushchev paid a state visit to Yugoslavia, Marshal Tito invited the Serbian patriarch to the diplomatic reception. Maybe they decided that the Russian pariarch should not in any way be treated lower than his Serbian counterpart. So when Pundit Nehru paid a state visit to the

Soviet Union, Patriarch Alexis was invited to the diplomatic reception. Since then it has been customary for the church to be represented at such occasions. This is an indication of the close co-operation of church and state. The church has increasingly co-operated with the regime in relation to countries where there are large Orthodox populations. The patriarch has criticized non-Communist governments for imperialism and lack of humanitarianism, without uttering a word of criticism against the Soviet Union's persecution of its ethnic minorities. The patriarch called upon the British Government to respect in Cyprus the right of self-determination for small nations. The patriarch also condemned the French and British invasion of Egypt while defending Soviet intervention in Hungary. These and similar acts absorbed the church more and more into the state and also laid further heavy demands upon it.

KHRUSHCHEV AND THE CHURCH

It would seem that under Bulganin the church enjoyed more freedom. Both he and Marshal Zhukov were less disposed to indulge in antireligious activities, especially against the Russian Orthodox Church. But when Khrushchev became the master of Russia's destiny, the heavy hand of the state fell upon the church. It looks as if he forgot his own decree of 1954. Toward the end of the decade of the fifties, the press launched a ruthless attack upon the church. The bishops and priests were accused of immoral living, misappropriation of funds, and excessive drinking. Their private lives were investigated and their wartime records closely scrutinized. Personal disclosures of the lives of the clergy were broadcast in a sensational manner. Nothing like this had appeared in the Soviet press since the thirties. Many churches and monasteries were closed down in the various parts of the country.

For once the church took a courageous stand in self-defense. In December of 1959 the Holy Synod issued a bold and forthright decree pronouncing wholesale excommunication of all apostates who had supplied the Communists with antireligious material and thereby committed acts of public blasphemy.

In 1960 Georgii Karpov, who had been for a long time in

charge of the church's affairs, was relieved of his job and replaced by Vladimir Kuroyedov, a specialist in Marxism-Leninism and party agitation and propaganda. Gradually junior officials were replaced by new ones. Khrushchev gave the signal for the harsh treatment of the church, because in his speeches he paid more attention to religious problems than his predecessors had done. Khrushchev had traveled widely in the country and may have been impressed by its vitality. He did not think religion would die by itself, and therefore more concerted action against the church was required than had been the case so far. Khrushchev as a boy was baptized in the church and had learned the Scriptures in the parish school. His constant preoccupation with the problems of church and religion may mean that he is in conflict with his own past, and also that the real rival of the Communist way of life is the Christian way.

THEOLOGICAL SCHOOLS

The church certainly faces grave problems. But the one concession which she extracted from the state has a prospect of ensuring its continued life in the future. That one concession is the opening of the theological schools. The existence of a theological school is an anomaly in a Communist state. It is a living challenge to the ideology and totalitarian control of the state. The theoretical possibility of receiving theological education becomes an actuality if there are theological schools.

In 1954-55 the Zagorsk seminary had 140 students for a four-year program. During the same period theological schools in Leningrad had 160 students, excluding those who were taking correspondence courses. In 1956 Odessa Seminary had 150 students. Some smaller seminaries had small numbers of students. One statement estimated that there were 1500 students in the whole of the Soviet Union. This appears to be an inflated figure. In 1960 only 155 new graduates of theological schools became parish priests. This is a very small number, but it does ensure orderly church life, and if the quality is good the loss from quantity can be mitigated. What kind of new bishop will arrive when the old veterans of persecutions have passed on? The episcopate was renewed under Patriarch Alexis by those who were either emigrés or children of emigrés. Additionally, bishops were promoted from the ranks of those priests who were trained at the theological faculty of Warsaw University or at the Paris Theological Institute.

The Communist Party and ideology claim authority over all of Soviet life. Its claims are totalitarian. The church, therefore, has to be watchful against political infiltration of its ranks. In a sense it will be difficult for the church to control such activity completely. Along with many genuine candidates for the ministry, there is every likelihood that some are enrolled to look after the interests of the party and report on the loyalty of the would-be clergy. The fear of such activity sows seeds of suspicion in the church and also makes believers uncertain about some priests. Some graduates of theological schools and even certain theological lecturers have turned renegades and have been exploited to the fullest extent to show the church in a bad light and to enhance the cause of militant atheism. These are the people who write the most sensational antireligious articles in the newspapers.

CHURCH PROPERTY AND FINANCE

The finances of the church seem to be in good shape again. The church is permitted to own property on a limited scale and also own means of production. A property-owning church is another anomaly in a Communist state. The churches can manufacture church vessels, vestments, altar bread, and icons. But the major portion of the church's income comes from the manufacture and sale of candles. These candles can be made inexpensively, but they are sold at very lucrative prices in the churches. Even the poorest of believers buys a candle or two, knowing that it goes to support the church. The standard of living of the priests even in the countryside has improved considerably. The church has to watch lest its growing wealth risk its spiritual life again.

The concordat between church and state is indeed a precarious affair. It can be turned off and on. Previous history bears witness to this. The Communist state regards the church as incompatible with it. It objects to the very existence of the church. The toleration toward the church can be ended at the command of the Communist Party. The intellectual starvation of the church is a patent fact. The publication of religious books is insignificant. There were only fifty thousand copies of the Russian translation of the Bible printed in 1956—two to a parish. The works of theological scholarship can only be copied and cannot be printed or mimeographed. This severely limits the church in fighting superstition and in containing its extremist sections. Yet, taking everything into account, the church has performed a heroic mission in the most difficult circumstances. Its liturgy and sacraments have consoled millions, and it has engendered so much spiritual power that mere terror and persecution cannot extinguish its light.

3

Christianity and Communism
(A Historical Connection)

Hegel's philosophy dominated the philosophic scene not only in Germany but also in England and America. It is a tribute to Hegel's universal genius that every philosophical movement of the late nineteenth and the early twentieth century has started as a criticism of his ideas. Marxism, existentialism, instrumentalism, and even philosophical analysis are all reactions to Hegelian or neo-Hegelian modes of thought.

SYSTEM AS A KEY

Hegel philosophized in a sweeping and synoptic manner. He did not consider things, people, and events in a piecemeal fashion; he saw all these and much more in a unified philosophic vision. As a matter of fact he regarded "the system" as the key to the understanding of reality. To him system was reality. That is why he was able to say "the real is the rational and the rational real." He did not mean that everything is neat. But the confusions, conflicting interests, and cross purposes are so handled by the "cunning of reason" that an ordered vision arises.

LOGIC AND DIALECTIC

Hegel was acutely sensitive to change and development in history. He found that Aristotelian logic was too static to account for changing events. He, therefore, abandoned it and proposed a more dynamic logic, substituting subject for substance. The earlier logic preoccupied itself with things and objects, where the new logic dealt with change and activity. Hegel's logic worked in a dialectical manner. It conceived contradiction as an agent of change. A given thesis developed itself into an antithesis and then both were resolved in a synthesis. This synthesis became in its turn a thesis, and the dialectical movement started again. This would go on throughout history till the Absolute Mind came to full and perfect self-consciousness. The dialectical method was a powerful interpretive instrument, also providing a philosophical justification for the Christian doctrine of providence. Hegel's intention invariably was to use logic to explain life, but in the course of applying logic to life, logic became too powerful for life and brought it under its aegis. The subsequent history of European thought shows that the dismemberment of the Hegelian system is due to the fact that there is no logic comprehensive enough to contain all the richness of life. Logic is not life, and when it is forced into that position, the logical structure cracks.

PRIMACY OF THE SPIRIT

History is autobiography of God. The Absolute Spirit initiates the historical process, and traversing its course through the multitudinous free forms of political, social, and religious existence, comes to full freedom which is its own full self-consciousness. Primacy and ultimacy belong to the Absolute.

According to Hegel, the Absolute came to full political awareness in the Prussian Germanic state, to full religious freedom in the Germanic Protestant Christianity, and to complete philosophic awareness in Hegel's own philosophy. This systematic suffocation became so acute that Kierkegaard had to cry out that he would not be "a paragraph in a system," and Karl Marx turned to revolutionary activity in revolt against theoretical construction.

LEFT-WING HEGELIANS

The young Hegelians were orthodox followers of their philosophic mentor in the beginning, but as they applied the dialectic of continuous change they were led to a revolutionary political philosophy which was closer to the French enlightenment than to Hegel. They applied a historical dialectical method to social institutions. In this they were superior to the enlightenment. The French materialist thinkers tried to refute religion by means of logic, whereas the radical Hegelians showed by the application of their historical method that instituions of politics and religion outgrow themselves by historical development.

Historical criticism was first applied to religion, particularly to the Scriptures of the Christian religion. The vigorous application of biblical criticism revealed that it had a deep relationship to the challenging of social and political institutions. When criticism raises doubts about religious authority, by implication every other kind of authority becomes questionable. Christianity emphasized its other-worldliness, and yet its emphasis on authority and tradition supported the status quo. The radical Hegelians wanted to discover the historical continuity of Christianity by subjecting its Scriptures and doctrines to the test of historical criticism.

David F. Strauss, Bruno Bauer, and Ludwig Feuerbach did precisely this from their respective points of view. Strauss, taking all the Gospels together, found them riddled with contradictions. To him, the Gospels were creations of the myth-making consciousness of the Christian community, and the life and activity of this community could be understood only in the light of Jewish religious history. Thus a believer came to know that his beliefs did not descend from "out there" but were a result of imminent historical process.

Bruno Bauer criticized Strauss for not fixing critically the priority of the Gospels in relation to one another. He showed that Mark was original and that the other three were just copies. Only an individual—never a community—could write a Gospel. He found the Gospel of Mark so self-contradictory as to be historically incredible. Bauer believed that he had knocked out the historical foundation of Christianity.

Ludwig Feuerbach embarked upon a radical reconstruction of Christianity. Believing that man is what he eats, he said that the basis of religion is emotion and not reason. What man likes and approves he idealizes; what he lacks he compensates for. Only a poor man can have a rich god. When the relation between man and nature is broken, he fills the gap by projecting a god. God is the idealization of man, just as theology is in fact anthropology.

From Strauss and Bauer to Feuerbach, Christianity was transformed from religion centered in God to a religion centered in man. This was not merely a methodological change, but a substantive change. It was no longer believed that to understand things divine one should start with men, but rather that if there were any God it was man. This is a radical reconstruction of Christianity.

FEUERBACH AND KARL MARX

During the formative years of 1841-1844 Marx was an enthusiastic Feuerbachian. Even when he had become critical of Feuerbach, he still acknowledged his indebtedness to him in generous terms. Feuerbach's thinking was of critical importance, because both Vissarion Belinsky and Karl Marx passed through it in their respective developments of Russian atheistic socialism and Western atheistic Marxism.

Marx, like Feuerbach, demanded a reconstruction of philosophy to deal with the practical problems of men. He joined Feuerbach in emphasizing that human beings are the carriers of cultural patterns in their empirical and social contexts; that traditional concepts of God, man, and the world are projections of the unconscious wishes of men.

Engels recorded his opinion that in spite of Feuerbach's emphasis on nature, things, and man, he was still caught up in abstractions. A bold step had to be taken beyond him. From the abstract man who became the focal point of Feuerbach's new reconstructed religion, a step had to be taken to the science of real men and their concrete, historical development. This carrying of Feuerbach beyond Feuerbach was done by Marx in 1845 in his book *The Holy Family*.

In the spring of 1845, Marx jotted down in his notebook eleven comments in the form of theses on the position of Feuerbach. Since these theses preceded Marx's formulation of his own position, they had a crucial and germinal importance for the devel-

opment of Marxism. We shall write down the eleven theses of
Marx on Feuerbach and add some comments at the end.

MARX'S THESES ON FEUERBACH

I

The chief defect of all hitherto existing materialism—that
of Feuerbach included—is that the object, reality, sensuousness, is conceived only in the form of the *object* or *contemplation* but not as *human sensuous activity practice,* not subjec-
tively. Thus it happened that the *active* side, in opposition to
materialism, was developed by idealism—but only abstractly,
since, of course, idealism does not know real sensuous activity as such. Feuerbach wants sensuous objects, really differ-
entiated from the thought-objects, but he does not conceive
human activity itself as activity *through objects.* Consequently, in the *Essence of Christianity,* he regards the theoretical attitude as the only genuinely human attitude, while
practice is conceived and fixed only in its dirty-Jewish form
of appearance. Hence he does not grasp the significance of
"revolutionary," of practical-critical, activity.

II

The question whether objective truth can be attributed to
human thinking is not a question of theory but is a practical
question. In practice man must prove the truth, i.e., the reality
and power, the "this-sidedness" of his thinking. The dispute
over the reality or non-reality of thinking which is isolated
from practice is a purely scholastic question.

III

The materialist doctrine that men are products of circumstances and upbringing and that, therefore, changed men are
products of other circumstances and changed upbringing, for-
gets that circumstances are changed precisely by men and that
the educator must himself be educated. Hence this doctrine
necessarily arrives at dividing society into two parts, of which
one towers above society (in Robert Owen, for example).

The coincidence of the changing of circumstances and of
human activity can only be conceived and rationally understood as revolutionising practice.

IV

Feuerbach starts out from the fact of religious self-aliena-
tion, the duplication of the world into a religious, imaginary
world and a real one. His work consists in the dissolution of
the religious world into its secular basis. He overlooks the fact

that after completing this work, the chief thing still remains to be done. For the fact that the secular foundation lifts itself above itself and establishes itself in the clouds as an independent realm is only to be explained by the self-cleavage and self-contradictoriness of this secular basis. The latter must itself, therefore, first be understood in its contradiction and then by the removal of the contradiction, revolutionised in practice. Thus, for instance, once the earthly family is discovered to be the secret of the holy family, the former must then itself be theoretically criticised and radically changed in practice.

V

Feuerbach, not satisfied with *abstract thinking,* appeals to *sensuous contemplation,* but he does not conceive sensuousness as a practical, human-sensuous activity.

VI

Feuerbach resolves the religious essence into the human. But the human essence is no abstraction in each single individual. In its reality it is the *ensemble* of the social relations.

Feuerbach, who does not attempt the criticism of this real essence, is consequently compelled:

1. To abstract from the historical process and to fix the religious sentiment as something for itself and to presuppose an abstract—*isolated*—human individual.

2. The human essence, therefore, can with him be comprehended only as "genus," as a dumb internal generality which merely *naturally* unites the many individuals.

VII

Feuerbach, consequently, does not see that the "religious sentiment" is itself a social product, and that the abstract individual whom he analyses belongs in reality to a particular form of society.

VIII

Social life is essentially *practical.* All mysteries which mislead theory to mysticism find their rational solution in human practice and in the comprehension of this practice.

IX

The highest point attained by contemplative materialism, i.e., materialism which does not understand sensuousness as practical activity, is the outlook of single individuals in "civil society."

X

The standpoint of the old materialism is "civil society";

the standpoint of the new is *human* society or socialised humanity.

XI

The philosophers have only *interpreted* the world in various ways; the point however is to *change* it.

Marx was deeply indebted to the materialism of Feuerbach. His criticism was that this was still an "ism" and that Feuerbach had not grasped the significance of practice (praxis). For Marx, theory was a guide to action, and practice was composed of the numerous activities necessary to test theory. Praxis was more comprehensive than practicality. It implied skills, technical procedures, know-how, and living traditions that man brought to bear up everything he did. That which the scientists actually did was scientific practice, and what the scientists performed was supported by the practices of the culture they lived in. Knowledge became power for man when it transformed things for the sake of social needs. For Marx, significance of any theory lay in what it enabled men to do or not to do.

Practice, he believed, tests truth. Marx rejected all kinds of idealism. To him the reality or non-reality of a theory apart from practice was scholastic hairsplitting. The truth of a theory depended upon whether it was conducive to the realization of predicted consequences. Marx emphasized will to action in order to test belief and also to find out if more evidence were needed for further action. Marx could not develop the full implications of his theory of truth. However, his main purpose was to provide guidance for the actions of the working class.

In Thesis III, Marx was contending against materialistic variety of utopian socialism. Marx thought Feuerbach was a utopian socialist. These socialists divided society into two groups: the common people who were the product of their circumstances, and the Robert Owen type of people who stood above the social process as if their views of social reform were not conditioned by their circumstances. Their ideals were free from historical conditioning and therefore equally applicable to all periods of history. These utopian socialists also thought that if their ideals had gained currency earlier, the course of social history would have been different. Marx, in contrast to the utopian socialists, emphasized the interaction between nature, society, and man. New productive forces created new needs, and to satisfy these needs new ideals were fashioned as instruments for the changing of society. The struggle to change institutions also changed the men who took part in the struggle. The praxis of changing society educated the workers. According to Marx, revolutionary activity and not mere criticism was the driving force of history, philosophy, and religion.

In Theses IV, VI, and VII, Marx was trying to show that Feuerbach's psychology of religion was abstract and inadequate. The elements which made man create a dreamy world of religions where the inequalities of real life were equalized and compensated for had a psychological ingredient, but actually they were sociological. The source of religion was to be found in the conflict between the ways men actually produced and the traditional ways under which production was carried—the antagonism between new needs and old ways. These conflicts led to a split in experience. One part of the division was idealized and formed the cultus and theology of religion, and the other was the everyday drab existence.

Marx contended that the changing of the economic order and its productive mechanism would eradicate the illusions of religion. This was, however, a presupposition, and it still remains to be seen whether or not the transformation of the economic order will ever eliminate religion. The point that Marx was making against Feuerbach was that theology is not only anthropology, but is really sociology. As to how the religious illusions arose, there did not seem to be a definitive analysis. Neither Marx nor any of his followers embarked upon a detailed analysis of various religions to prove their point. Analyses by Max Weber, E. Troeltsch, and R. H. Tawney are available, but they are not from the Marxian point of view. It seems that a phrase coined by Marx under the influence of Feuerbach carries the weight of arguments and analyses: "Religion is the opiate of the people." From the history of the use of this sentence it would appear that the followers of Marx have been doped by it insofar as they think this is the last word on religion.

Thesis V picked up the theme of the first thesis and gave credit to Feuerbach for identifying reality with sensibility. The idealists identified reality with thought. However, Marx criticized Feuerbach's description of the identification of reality with sensibility as being too ideational and not empirical. In other words, Feuerbach, although a materialist and a good one at that, was still a philosopher of the idea of materialism. Marx did not consider sensations to be results of the actions of things upon the bodies. The body, to Marx, was not passive, so the sensations were effects of the actions of things on active bodies. The sensations were, therefore, interactions. Marx gave sensations a social interpretation. He said that in a common environment individuals drawn from different cultures would make different reactions. They would act and see selectively and describe their reactions differently. Hunger is a natural phenomenon, but the way in which man satisfies his hunger is a social fact. Social organization, he felt, modified physical environment, and through the application of industry that which was naturally given was socially taken.

In Thesis VIII Marx spelled out his guiding principle. Marx did not admit the existence of insoluble problems nor did he concede that there were any mystical solutions. Mystical and irrational solutions were proposed for problems when their social context was not taken into account seriously. The social context was constituted not only by the immediate social needs which directed the course of scientific research but also by social habits and by modes of thought and action involved in communication. Fundamental concepts were not independent of experience. As a matter of fact, it should be shown how they were related to concrete situations, just as they came out of specific empirical activities. The relation between theory and practice, said Marx, is distorted if their social context is ignored.

Theses IX and X spell out the difference between old materialism and new materialism. Old materialism or contemplative materialism was advocated by Feuerbach and Jeremy Bentham. The concept of society according to the old materialism was atomistic. Its individuals were motivated by self-interest, and they entered into contractual arrangements with each other to protect their self-interest. The new materialism which was advocated by Marx centered on social interest—the interest of society. Social interest defines individual interest. Marx therefore required a collective control of all institutions which affected the life of man. This is what Marx meant by "socialised humanity."

The much-quoted Thesis XI illustrates the difference between Feuerbach and Marx, between philosophical activity as thinking of ideas, and revolutionary activity resulting in social change. In reply to Max Stirner's criticism of Feuerbach's philosophic position, the latter had characterized himself neither as an idealist nor as a materialist, but simply as a *man,* and, since man was man in society, as a communal man, which meant a Communist. Marx used this self-characterization of Feuerbach to point out his limitation. Feuerbach was a good philosopher, but practical activity was foreign to his philosophy. Marx considered his advance beyond Feuerbach to consist in the introduction of revolutionary activity, instead of mere thinking activity, as an agent of social change—a combination of thought and revolutionary action which would change the world. In going beyond Feuerbach, Marx had to learn from and depend upon him. Feuerbach taught Marx the meaning of realistic materialism.

FROM CHRISTIANITY TO MARXISM

In retrospect, we can see how young Christian thinkers schooled in Hegelian thought became radical Hegelians, and by applying historical and sociological criticism to the Scriptures, rendered them human—free of myth, miracle, and divinity. In the same manner, doctrines of God and of the divinity of Christ were shown to be the projections of human wishes and desires. Christianity was transformed into a theology, the positive meaning of which was anthropology. But man was not abstract man but social man, or socialized humanity. Hence Christianity was transfomed by Christians via materialism into Marxism. Marx, of course, performed the crowning act, just as Belinsky and others had started the internal Russianization of communism.

MARXISM

Lenin asserted that the teaching of Karl Marx was all powerful because of its truth. Marx presented a close-knit and well-rounded view of the world from which superstition and reactionary thought had been eliminated. According to Lenin, Marx was the inheritor of the best that nineteenth-century humanity produced.

So Marxism as an integrated view incorporates the best in German philosophy, English economic thought, and French social-ism. These are the three sources and constituent parts of Marxism. Marxism is materialism, but not of the eighteenth-century variety. Marx improved upon it and enriched it by taking over from the German classical philosophy of Hegel its most important element, the *dialectic*. Dialectic is the understanding of the process of evolu-tion in its most comprehensive and universal meaning. Dialectic assures knowledge of human relativity and the ever changing forms of matter. The discoveries of science confirm it and are explained by it. Dialectical materialism is the highest stage of arrival, and any new ways of bourgeois philosophers are simply a return to rotten idealism.

Marx developed dialectical materialism as an instrument for the understanding of nature into a tool for the understanding of human society. Marx developed a systematic and scientific theory of history, politics, and economics, thereby dispelling confusion and chaos from these areas of knowledge and activity. Lenin main-tained that just as man's knowledge of nature discloses an inde-pendent and developing process of nature, so also the social under-standing of men's views regarding religion, philosophy, and politics, etc., reflects the economic structure of society. Economics is the basis of politics. The European governments show the class prejudice in the organization of their states. States enforce the privileges of the bourgeoisie over against the proletariat. Lenin emphasized that the highly developed dialectical materialism of Marx had put the greatest instrument of understanding at the dis-posal of humanity in general and of the working class in particular.

Realizing that economics is the basis of politics, Marx devoted most of his energies to the study of the economic structure of society. Therefore, *The Capital* is devoted to the study of capitalist society. England being at the time the most highly developed capi-talist country, Marx studied closely the writings of Adam Smith and David Ricardo. Lenin maintained that Marx continued the work of these men, especially developing their labor theory of value most firmly and consistently.

The understanding of the labor theory of value is that the value of a commodity is defined by the quantity of labor time that has gone into its production. Marx contended that labor did not get its return for the full working day. A part of the working day earned labor and its return in the form of wages; the other part of the day went to the formation of profit for the capitalist, so labor worked part of the day for nothing but to create surplus value for the capitalist. It is the doctrine of surplus value which Lenin considered the keystone of Marx's economic theory.

In *The Capital,* Marx traced the development of economic theory and practice from simple barter to large-scale production. He showed how economically well-placed classes had exploited the serfs, laborers, and workers. Many kinds of socialist doctrines emerged to register protests against oppression and to find a new way. Even utopian socialism could not point a way out. According to Lenin, it was the genius of Marx who traced out in advance of others what the history of the world was leading to—the doctrine of class war. People are always stupid and fall prey to self-deception in politics until they one day find out that behind every moral, religious, political, or social declaration lies hidden the special interest of this or that class. Those who cry and work for reform will be fooled by the tactics of those who defend old regimes or institutions, until they find out that every one of these institutions is backed by the forces and interests of a dominant class or classes.

The only way to break the power of these dominant classes is to unite and organize for struggle those groups and forces in society who have been downtrodden, but are still capable of standing up and overthrowing the old and making way for the new. Only the dialectical materialism of Karl Marx, said Lenin, had shown to the proletariat the way out of the slavery in which all the oppressed had been caught. Only the economic theory of Marx had pinpointed the actual situation of the working classes in the general pattern of capitalism.

We have followed the lead of Lenin in describing Marxism, its contribution and greatness, and its indebtedness to the West in philosophy, economics, and social theory. Lenin was quite emphatic about the elements of indebtedness, although the trend of Marxist apologetics has been to declare Marxism free from any Western dependence.

Dialectic is that which unites the opposites. In the system of Hegel, the Absolute was comprehensive thought and experience. It covered the full course of history. The dialectic covers not only thought but also the temporal passage of events. The Absolute, which for Hegel had the significance of God, unfolded itself progressively from the lower forms of primitive society and religion to the highest forms of German state organization and Christianity. The key that unlocks the secret of this development is the dialectic. It should be pointed out that Hegel used the dialectical method to past historical operations; Marx, in contrast to Hegel, extended the dialectic to the future. Marx made the dialectic an instrument of prophecy. Karl Popper was right when he said that as long as Marx limited himself to institutional analysis, his judgments, even though one-sided, were both permanent and significant; but when he ventured on prophetic conclusions based upon the observation of the contemporary economic situation, he invariably failed. And the reason for his failure as a prophet lay in his making mandatory for the future what he observed in the present. Everything is possible in history, but to determine a rigid outcome, as if a precise scientific law of dialectical progress were at work, is bad science and poor prophecy.

The followers of Marx became dominated by the dialectic as an instrument of prophecy, thereby discouraging and side-stepping the belief that through the use of reason the world may be changed. Popper pronounced the judgment that scientific Marxism was dead, but the feeling of social responsibility which it aroused was sound and should be kept alive.

LENINISM

Stalin said that when you update Marxism to the period of capitalist imperialism and the proletarian revolution, it becomes Leninism. Lenin appeared at a time when Russia was getting ready for a revolution. It was therefore necessary for him to lead his followers in a revolutionary situation. Caught as he was in this situation, his main concern was not to iron out the fine points of Marxist theory, but to meet the practical demands of a situation which did not require that he should justify his policy theoretically, but that he should persuade his followers to pursue his policy. He possessed an uncanny instinct for grasping a situation, and justified his tactics by appeal to Marxist texts.

Lenin was dedicated to the revolutionary mission of the working classes and was a firm believer in Marx, although he had to exegete the writings of Marx in the light of the situations with which he was confronted. It is difficult to show how else Marx could have been interpreted. How could the revolution have occurred if Lenin had not interpreted Marx in the manner in which he did? The question of the relationship of ideology and power which is implied here shall be raised and discussed later.

CONTRIBUTIONS OF LENIN

Lenin made striking contributions to the strategy and tactics of revolution. He arrived too late in Russia to affect the course of the 1905 revolution, a spontaneous revolution of the masses which affected every level of society and forced different groups to sharpen their point of view.

Bolsheviks and Mensheviks met separately and together to iron out their respective stands and their attitude toward participation in the Duma. The differences between these two groups were mainly of tactics and not so much of principles. Both agreed that the 1905 revolution should be of the bourgeoisie, which would establish the capitalist order. The proletarian revolution demanded this as its first condition. They should not participate in government because this would alienate the middle class as well as the masses.

Lenin agreed with this, but maintained that for bringing about such a revolution the bourgeoisie would have to be revolutionary, and this was not the case in Russia. The proletariat must therefore be leaders in what had to be a bourgeois revolution, and co-operate with the bourgeoisie in the formation of government. Revolution, he maintained, must be democratic. It would be the democratic dictatorship of the proletariat and peasantry. Here he had already innovated beyond Marx. Trotsky added to this the element of proletarian revolutions in other countries to help the proletarian revolution in Russia, since Russia was mostly peasant.

The Mensheviks rejected both of these views. They held firmly that Marx had taught that the bourgeois revolution would occur first and the proletarian would follow it. They also rejected the view of Trotsky. But the Mensheviks were in no position to bring about a revolution. The two groups fought and disagreed with each other till 1914.

In 1920, Lenin said that the revolution of 1917 would have been impossible without the dress rehearsal of 1905. His analysis was that the proletariat needed the help of the peasantry, which came too late. The liberals betrayed the workers when it came to fighting. Lenin was deeply convinced that if the proletariat were to rise in revolt again, with the right support, nothing on earth could defeat them.

Series of events happened before the October revolution of 1917. The czar abdicated on March 15, whereas a provisional government had been formed a day before. However, on March 12 the Petrograd Soviet came into existence, and similar soviets were formed in each town and village, thereby creating the seat of dual and rival authority. Mensheviks controlled the town and social revolutionaries the village soviets. They had both agreed to co-operate with the provisional government.

Lenin returned to Petrograd on April 16 and immediately issued instructions to the Bolsheviks not to co-operate with the Government, but to establish a soviet republic to prepare the way for the government of the proletariat, and to nationalize land which the peasants were already appropriating. It is evident that Lenin turned away from parliamentarianism although he did not immediately advocate the overthrow of the Government. Lenin correctly sensed the mood of the masses as well as the fact that coalition government would fail—which it did.

The Government could not give the masses what they wanted, and Mensheviks and social revolutionaries were compromised because of their coalition with the Government. Lenin had advocated that all power go to the soviets, and now by offering peace, liberty, food, and land to the masses, he proclaimed the dictatorship of the proletariat and the peasants. The masses rose in angry revolt, the armed forces killed each other, and the Government lost all control. The Bolsheviks, small but well organized and led, seeing that the time had come, struck and seized power by a bloodless revolution. It is quite evident that the tactics of Lenin landed the Mensheviks in particular in a tight spot. They had done much to foment the revolution, and they had worked hard to establish soviets in every military unit, thus eroding the army from the inside.

The Mensheviks were probably right in thinking that Russia was not ready for the Marxist type of revolution, but Lenin took the chance anyhow. His ideas of public administration were simple and straightforward; he controlled a party which was a little bit better organized than any of the contenders, and he believed that although Russia was not quite ready for the proletarian revolution, Europe was nevertheless ripe for a social order.

It is possible to say that Lenin made the revolution as much as the revolution made him. In bringing about the revolution under the circumstances which prevailed in Russia at the time, Lenin was forced to forge a highly controlled and centralized party. The party was undemocratic in its structure, and inconsistent with the ideas of Western socialism. Marx had contended that a socialist society could be established only in a highly industrialized and developed country. The contention still remains to be proved, but Lenin short-circuited the process.

STATE AND REVOLUTION

Just before the revolution, Lenin published his most famous book, *State and Revolution*. In this book he tried to explain what Marx and Engels meant by the state and the "withering away" of the state. Positively he expounded his doctrine of the "dictatorship of the proletariat." This dictatorship was a new form of government which would follow the destruction of the capitalist state by the revolution.

Lenin interpreted Engels in the following manner. First, when Engels said that the revolution would put an end to the state and that the state would wither away, these were not one and the same thing, but two distinct matters. The abolition of the state meant the end of the bourgeois state, but the withering away of the state was quite different. It implied that this problem would occur in due course of time. This appears, on the face of it, to be something different from Engels' view. It is certainly clear that if this was Engels' meaning, he did not make it plain.

Lenin was warning his followers that the state would not end with the revolution but would continue in the form of the dictatorship of the proletariat. It would be temporary, and under it human exploitation would end. In the meantime, however, it would have to perform the coercive functions of the state, but these functions would be carried on by a majority instead of by a minority as earlier. The workers would be paid according to their work and not according to their need. He extended the doctrine of class struggle to the dictatorship of the proletariat.

The dictatorship of the proletariat would bring about democracy, but this does not imply parliamentarianism. He identified parliamentarianism with bourgeois democracy. Proletarian democracy was the organization of the exploited masses which enabled them to govern themselves in every possible way. Bourgeois democracy was for the rich, and its pretensions about the poor were hypocritical. He claimed that the proletarian democracy had the widest possible base, and therefore was far more representative than bourgeois democracy would ever be.

The point of proletarian democracy was that it represented the one and only class that there was. The corollary that followed from one-class society was naturally one-party system of government. Two-party system would imply at least two classes of people with two divergent and hostile interests. When the cause of division was removed there would remain one class and no conflict of interest.

We have noticed two steps in the tactics of Lenin. The first step was that the proletariat would join with the bourgeoisie, and the second that the bourgeoisie would be eliminated and there would be a dictatorship of the proletariat, or better still, proletarian democracy would rule supreme.

According to this principle, the soviets began to conduct the administration of the state, and within two years the administrative machinery was compounded with confusion. The result was that the soviets were pushed in the background and the party took over. The transfer from the soviets to the party was conducted by enabling party members to be successful at elections and appointed to key positions. Also, the state control of industry was placed in the hands of the party members. The vanguard of the proletariat was the party, and the party was the centralized and highly disciplined organ. This looks un-Russian, but Lenin knew that in order to bring about a revolution you would have to have a highly disciplined party, and Stalin followed him mercilessly. The majority should submit to minority. The party should be controlled by the central committee, which should have the power to purge unreliable elements.

"War communism" had taught him some lessons, and his emphasis on the party took him beyond what he expressed in *State and Revolution*. Lenin remained to the very last in favor of the "narrow" as against the "open" party, and Stalin followed him in this.

In the strategy and tactics for the advancement of communism abroad, Lenin advised that proletarian revolutionaries must combine strictest loyalty to Communist doctrines with flexibility to compromise as situations arose. To reject compromise on principle was foolish. Agitation and propaganda should go on, but that was not enough. The party was the vanguard of the millions, and it was on those millions that the revolution depended. Communist parties everywhere should strive to capture power, and in order to do this they could make and unmake agreements, perform zigzags or retreats, or take two steps backward in order to take one step forward.

In the all-important task of capturing power, the real enemies of the Communists are not only the right wing, but also the Socialists who compete with them for the allegiance of the workers. The forming of joint fronts with the Socialist becomes a necessity, and requires a great deal of ingenuity, because the Socialists are well aware of the aims of the Communists. The Communists, using the technique of the joint front, infiltrate minority and left-wing groups for the purpose of exploiting the interests of others to advance their own course. Whenever they can manage, they see to it that the president of an organization is politically colorless and socially prominent, but that the secretary, who exercises real control, is either a Communist or a crypto-Communist.

CAPITALIST IMPERIALISM

It is said that Lenin's doctrine of capitalist imperialism constitutes an advance on Marxist economics. Imperialism is the continuation of capitalism to the stage where monopoly and finance capital become dominant, where surplus capital is available for foreign export, where the world has been carved off into spheres of interest, and where colonial territories have been acquired. In this stage, big banks and financial corporations have taken over from the original industrialist. Imperialism is "monopoly capitalism" and it cannot progress beyond that stage. It is its decadent stage. The class war extends to this period because the dialectical end of imperialism is socialism.

Lenin was the architect of the party. He developed its tactics and strategy for internal and international purposes. He guided the 1917 revolution. He could not do it by following literally what Marx had written; he had to learn the hard way from concrete situations and then justify his actions by the exegesis of Marx's writings. He could not proceed from the text to the situation but only from the situation to the text. This raises very acutely the question of the relation between Communist ideology and power. This we shall discuss after we have noted Stalin's contribution to Communist theory and practice.

STALIN

Stalin continued in the manner of Lenin. He also was guided by circumstances to give direction to Marxist thought. Just as Lenin invoked Marx, so was Stalin careful to appeal to the authority of Lenin. With Stalin one very important thing happened. The czars were dead and gone, but Stalin gave to the Russian people under a different name an autocracy of Byzantine variety. The

Russian people in their long history have only known an authoritarian and totalitarian form of government. This was a continuation of it into a new period with new methods and policies.

SOCIALISM IN ONE COUNTRY

Socialism in one country was the main contention between Stalin and Trotsky. Trotsky maintained that Europe was ripe for socialist revolution and this should be given priority. Stalin was not as convinced of the ripeness of Europe as Trotsky was. He felt there would be considerable opposition to revolution in European countries. Moreover, he was convinced of the specious genius of the Russian people and wanted Russia to be the first to realize the new social order. It looks as if the quarrel between Stalin and Trotsky was the new version of the Slavophile-Western controversy. Trotsky lost and Stalin won. The Russian masses were happy to know that their country was strong enough to realize socialism at home, and at the same time the emphasis on socialism in one country implied that it was not intended for export. This latter may have mollified international opinion somewhat.

Stalin achieved power as an organizer. Since at that time organization was of primary importance, he became very good at it, so much so that he centralized unlimited powers in the central organs of the party such as Politbureau and the Secretariat. The party became less proletarian and more bureaucratic. Lenin certainly did not advocate a government of this type. Also, the collectivization of agriculture which resulted in the expropriation of the *Kulaks* is a departure from Lenin. But these are the consequences of the doctrine of socialism in one country. Stalin also denounced equalitarianism by using the authority of Engels. Equality, declared Stalin, does not mean that individual requirements and individual lives should be equalized. It means that the classes should be abolished. However, Stalin maintained, when transition is made to communism, then men will be paid and compensated according to their needs. However, the determination of what the needs are will be the responsibility of the state.

NATIONALISM

The doctrine of socialism in one country was designed to make Russia the leader of world revolution. The more successful the revolution became, the more Russian national interests were involved in it. Soviet power gradually ceased to be a means to revolutionary purpose and became an end in itself, so much so that identification between Soviet power and Russian power took place. The idea of communism merged with the idea of nationalism. Peter the Great and Ivan the Terrible became the heroes of the Soviet Union, and Suvorov and Kutusov, the generals of the czars, became the military shining lights of Soviet history. In Stalin's time, particularly up to 1948, the combination of nationalism and communism helped the Russian state and the Communist revolution.

But this combination also contained the seeds of division in the Communist movement, based on divergent national interests. The first indication of trouble in the Communist household was the defection and ouster of Yugoslavia in 1948. At the present time it is the major problem in the Communist world. The doctrine of socialism in one country has openly divided the Communist countries, and we are current witnesses to what has happened between Russia and China.

Stalin engineered inconspicuously the transfer of Lenin's power to himself. Shortly after the civil war he became Commissar of Nationalities, the Commissar of Workers' and Peasants' Inspectorate, and a member of the Politbureau. Later he became the Secretary General and made the power of the Politbureau dependent upon his own office. It is said that if the will and testament of Lenin had been made public and its instructions had been followed, Stalin would have been of no consequence for the future of Russia and world history.

Four months after the death of Lenin the testament was read to the plenary session of the Central Committee. When the contents were divulged there were red faces and general embarrassment. Stalin looked small and miserable in his seat. At this terrible moment, Zinoviev saved the day for Stalin by rising and saying that in respect to Stalin Lenin's fears were wrong. Kamenev also appealed, and by forty votes to ten it was decided not to publish Lenin's will, but to leave Stalin in power. Zinoviev and Kamenev soon found out and so did the other rivals of Stalin that Lenin was right after all, but it was too late in the day to be able to do anything about it. It is in this manner that one of the greatest but least dramatized shifts of absolutist power took place in recent history.

POWER AND IDEOLOGY

Marx constantly emphasized the interrelation of theory and practice. This was one of his major reasons for departing from Feuerbach, and it was the same reason that made him reverse the course of Hegelian philosophy and stand Hegel on his head. However, significant power developments took place under Lenin and Stalin and in Soviet history subsequent to Stalin. This prompts the question of the relation between theory and practice or ideology and power. Has Marxism been in effect superceded by the power dynamics of later history, or has a more subtle and less obvious relationship developed between Communist ideology and power?

It seems that among close students of Russian affairs there are differences of opinion on this very vital subject. Professor Rostow maintains that in the complex phenomenon of the relationship between ideology and power the balance has shifted in favor of power. Although the personalities of the holders of power are very important in the exercise thereof, Rostow does not study Russian power from the psychological point of view. He bases his concept on the priority of power and on a complex relation between Marx's idea that historical events take a determinable form and Lenin's conception of the Communist Party as the vehicle of the realization of what Marx had predicted about history.

The party gains legitimacy and the right to prescribe the "correct line" of action. This implies that even if the majority and the proletariat wished otherwise, the party, knowing the "correct line," can dictate its will. Often it means that the dominant personality of the leader of the party charts out the course of action. Since the difference between the party and the majority can be arguable, it leads to more and more acquisition of power by the party. In other words, the party takes on a conspiratorial role, and when the national situation is confused—as was the case in Russia both before and after the revolution—the role of the party becomes more dictatorial and power begins to be vested completely in one person or in a handful of them. Even in czarist times, a conspiratorial role was attractive to the reformers, who, because of economic, political, and social frustrations, tried to overthrow by force the czarist government.

The emergence of the priority of power arises due to the convergence of Russian and Communist conspiratorial factors and to the personal characteristics of the Soviet leaders. Those men come to the forefront who have respect for power, take risks to achieve it, and know how to use it. Those who are unable to resolve the conflict between their idealism and power position are eliminated. Professor Rostow does not want his position to be understood as a clear-cut case of power versus ideology. Some elements of ideology carry a power ingredient with them, such as the nationalization of industry; others, such as the placing of political power in the hands of trade unions and the soviets, conflict with it.

The consistency in the inner story of Russian communism lies in the fact that the life of the nation and of the organizations in it has been organized in such a way as to put the overwhelming balance of power in the hands of the party as Lenin had conceived it. The use of this power by Lenin and Stalin was different. There was more cultural freedom. Freedom of discussion in the party was permitted unless it constituted a serious challenge. Lenin was unwilling to use the death penalty against fellow Communists. Lenin gave priority to power over other goals; Stalin was more consistent in the use of power and less hampered by considerations other than power. Stalin extended the role of power by creating new organizations on a vast scale. It can be said that he created a bureaucracy of absolute power.

The application of the principle of the priority of power created new situations, leading to consequences which were not predictable and determinable and therefore not under the control of the Soviet regime. The Marxist declarations which stood Hegel on his head were through the use and extension of power of the state under Lenin, but Stalin led to the reinstatment of Hegel with regard to state power. Russian communism is a single-minded use of the immense powers of a modern state by a small group to reorganize the vast spectrum of national life. Professor Rostow maintains that the de facto ideology of the Soviet Union is that the *great leader* and the *state* are the two main forces of history, rather than the economic forces or even the combination of economic, political, and cultural forces. Judging by the normative principle that the history of a society is an interacting process, the actual course of a national history is not determined solely by the power-political factor.

The actual history, therefore, of Soviet society is an interaction between the aims of its rulers, the position of Russia in relation to its geography and natural resources, the stage of political and economic development, and the cultural forces in Russian history which by their nature are only capable of slow change. Therefore, the forms which the pursuit of power has created have been determined by the slow-changing realities of the Russian scene rather than by the ideological considerations. Lenin said that the Russian peasant was a product of countless generations that preceded, and he could not be changed in a hurry. He had to be taken as he was and then worked upon. The Soviet rulers have taken the Russian people as they are and then applied power controls to extract from them efficiency and conformity. This pragmatic handling of the Russian people has Russianized the forms of Communist dictatorship. However, Professor Rostow maintains that taking on Russian mannerisms does not mean that the interests of Soviet rulers and the interests of the Russian nation and people have become identical.

Soviet Russia teaches a lesson about the awesomeness of totalitarian power, and also teaches that even the maximum use of political power has cultural limitation. Above all, it teaches that limitation which the resistance of men can offer even though that resistance may be passive.

Professor Carew Hunt maintains that even now theory and ideology play a great role. He says everybody agrees that ideology was crucial in the prerevolutionary period when Bolsheviks were literally fed on it, and that in the decade after the revolution the workers were inspired by doctrine in changing the shape of their country. But after 1930, when Stalin gained absolute power, this situation changed. The mechanism of state and secret police was so enormously strengthened that any chance of a classless society was remote. With the Stalin-Hitler pact and World War II, Russia entered upon an era of sheer power play. It is, therefore, concluded by some that ideology does not play an effective role in Communist designs and actions, but only serves as a window dressing. Only a few fanatics believe in the ideology; as a general rule no one else does—least of all the leaders. Professor Hunt feels that such conclusions are unjustified and that statements to that effect are wrong.

Professor Hunt argues that the ordinary Soviet citizen is constantly subjected to skillful doctrinal propaganda. He is taught that the ideology on which the Soviet Union is based makes it the envy of the rest of the world. The Western nations are jealous of it and have surrounded the Soviet Union in order to destroy it. The Soviet leadership wants its people to be saturated by this ideology, and those who occupy sensitive positions have to pass through graded schools of doctrinal instruction. It is significant to observe that whenever the leadership is in a tight spot—the examples of which are de-Stalinization and intervention in Hungary—they appeal to first principles of Communist ideology. The hard-headed Soviet leaders would not emphasize indoctrination if it did not pay off. Also, it is a plain fact that when an ideology is constantly directed at people without contest and challenge it is bound to affect them. The Soviet people do not have to be totally committed to it to know that there is something in it which has made their nation great and powerful.

What about the Soviet leadership? It is difficult to assess what the top-ranking Soviet leaders believe, but it should be borne in mind that no leadership group finds it difficult to believe in that which gives them the power. The Soviet leadership is no exception —indeed they have been fed on the ideology from their very birth.

The leadership is confident that history is on their side and that capitalist bourgeoisie will collapse and the Communist proletariat will be the victor. Democratic governments often mention practical advantages and disadvantages as reasons for policy recommendations. This is not the way it happens in the Soviet Union. The usual procedure is that articles will appear in *Pravda* justifying the fact that the recommended new policy is in accord with the teaching of Lenin or is consistent with the decisions of party congresses. As to how far it is ideology and not practical advantage, this is difficult to determine. The analysts who advocate that the leaders of the Kremlin act only on the basis of power politics and use ideology as subterfuge for this purpose are also hard put to distinguish clearly between the power and ideology elements of the mixture.

Professor Hunt stresses that inefficiency is a sign that ideology is operative. He says that waste would be avoided if small traders were permitted to operate on profit. The fishmonger who does not now put his fish on ice would certainly do so if he had incentive, but profit-making would refute Communist ideology and hence it cannot be permitted.

Another example of inefficiency due to ideology is that Soviet agriculture would be more efficient if the Machine Tractor Stations were handed over to the collective farms.* But in ideological status, the Machine Tractor Stations, being fully state-owned, are higher than the collective farms. Ideology demands that higher forms of socialization cannot be submitted to a lower form.

The dogmatism in the Soviet foreign policy is also a result of Communist ideology. When the Soviet Union enters into diplomatic relations with non-Communist countries, they promise that there will be no interference in the internal affairs of the countries. But Communist ideology advocates that non-Communist governments should be overthrown by all and any means. This prospect no government can accept. There is, therefore, a cleavage between Communist and non-Communist countries, and Communist ideology is responsible for it. Sheer power politics would not be able to explain this cleavage. The Soviet Union is a powerful state and in the executing of its policies there is the play of power politics, but

* Khrushchev has already recommended this.

this does not deny the force of ideology. The case may be that it is exceedingly difficult to disassemble the parts that are ideological from those of power politics.

Professor Z. K. Brzezinski advocates a middle position, saying that ideology is an action program in which strategies that look at the larger purpose and end of history are combined with tactics that apply to local, particular, and national situations. The larger view gives the adherents of communism a consistent and long-range way of looking at affairs. It also has the temptations to make them dogmatic and rigid. Western statesmen, with the possible exception of De Gaulle, look at events and their issues more pragmatically. They do not work with a larger view of things. In Brzezinski's view, the errors of Suez in 1956 and of Cuba in 1961 were largely due to a lack of understanding of the larger context of international affairs. These were not individual cases which, on the basis of the case-study method, could be disposed of by a blow from the outside. In the case of Nasser, a political and historical understanding of Arab nationalism was required. Nasser had eliminated the middle groups and brought the masses close to himself. He could not be defeated by a blow from outside because there was nothing to assist that blow from inside. Similarly, Castro could only be understood from the angle of left-wing revolution, and this could be met only by the organization of the democratic left, not right and center.

To the question of whether or not ideology will inevitably lead to dogmatic and therefore historical mistakes, Brzezinski answers that it depends upon the content of ideology. As far as nazism was concerned, its dogmatism not only made its rank and file followers irrational, but also blinded its leaders. The Communists by their emphasis on tactics possess a sense of the reality of political and social situations which will temper their irrationalism. He maintains that although as a rule nonideological Western leaders react more pragmatically and Communist ideological leaders act more dogmatically, it does not follow abstractly that the former will be more rational than the latter. Pragmatic considerations also play their part in the ideology of communism.

We have noticed that all the three positions make their distinctive emphases, but at the same time they all recognize to a degree the difficulty of extricating ideology from power. However, the one-party dictatorship without creative dialogue and criticism increases the chances of dogmatism. It could be that the pluralization of the Communist movement may correct it to some extent, but this will require a major change in the movement.

4

Christianity and Democracy

The Reformation created circumstances for the birth of the modern state. The "priesthood of all believers" and the "liberty of the Christian man" were revolutionary ideas, but by themselves they could not change the state of affairs. The absolutism of the papacy could be challenged and overthrown only if the interests of the princes and kings coincided with the ideals of the Reformation. The kings and princes of the sixteenth century were deeply interested in deposing the political overlordship of the pope. The combination of the spiritual power of the Reformation and the political power of kings and princes achieved its purpose, but by the same token the effective control over the lives of the people of Europe passed from the clerical to the political. The secular state which is so well known to us now was born at that time.

WARS OF RELIGION

The wars of religion beween Catholics and Protestants in the sixteenth and seventeenth centuries determined the primacy of the political over the religious and the ascendency of the state over religion. This is the exact opposite of the state of affairs which existed in medieval Christendom. These wars of religion became so acute that they nearly jeopardized the very existence of Western civilization. It was no wonder that the minds of men strayed away from Christianity to more rallying issues of nationality, state, and politics.

France, in the sixteenth century, is perhaps the place where the course of these wars can be best chartered and their outcome determined. The Catholics and the Huguenots fought an internecine warfare. The issues were the centralized power of the monarchy versus provincial privileges and independence of the cities and of the nobility. The Protestant Huguenots were on the side of pluralism and constitutionality over against the monarchy. This was definitely the wrong side to be on in the France of that day. But then a terrible event took place in 1572—the St. Bartholomew Massacre. Many Huguenot gentlemen had come to Paris to celebrate the marriage of Henry, king of Navarre, to Margaret, and to take part in the festivities accompanying the event. The marriage took place on August 18, and on August 22 the Huguenot Admiral De Coligny was shot from a window as he was approaching his lodging place. He lost a finger and suffered a broken arm and was confined to his bed. On August 24, the day of the feast of St. Bartholomew, when church bells were ringing, the Catholic Duke of Guise led his men to the house of the admiral. The men spiked him and threw his body in the street where it was disgraced and badly mutilated. Then the general massacre of the Huguenots followed. It is said that several thousand were killed in Paris alone.

As a result of the massacre and general reflection on depopulation and impoverishment of France caused by the civil war, much serious political thought was aroused. The monarchy benefitted the most. It secured itself against papal infringement and benefitted from the Calvinist principle of passive obedience to royal authority. The Jesuit writers gave up the direct defense of the supremacy of the pope and argued for indirect supremacy. They went on emphasizing the point on which the Huguenots lost, i.e., some kind of pluralism and constitutionalism. There was, however, a very important political gain. It came to be accepted that the religion of the monarch is not obligatory for his subjects. The Edict of Nantes embodied the principle of toleration permitting a religious minority to exist when the monarch and the majority of the population are of different religious persuasions. The removal of the overlordship of the pope raised the question of the right of the kings. The divine right of kings was a protection against both the pope and the people.

A significant event was the emergence of a third political party called the "Politiques." The name implied that the members of this group acted from motives of policy rather than principle. They were Catholics, and when called upon bore arms for the king, but they were opposed to all coercion in religious matters. The most enlightened interpreter of this view was Chancellor L'Hopital. He advocated that words such as "Lutheran," "Huguenot," and "papist" are devilish because they create faction and sedition. He advised that the word "Christian" be kept unadulterated. He emphasized that even if a man is excommunicated, he still remains a citizen.

The Politiques were moderate and utilitarian. They grasped the fundamental reality of the sixteenth century—that the loss of religious unity was irreparable, but the unity of state and nationality could be saved. In their political thinking they were nationalists. They strove hard to save the unity of France from the wreckage of religious wars. This does not mean they did not appreciate the value of a unified religion, but they knew from hard experience that this was not within their reach. They settled for what could be salvaged. They were accused by their opponents of preferring the stability of the state and of their homes to the salvation of their souls, or of preferring the peace of the kingdom without God rather than the challenge of being at war alongside of him. Jean Bodin fully supports the policy of toleration advocated by the Politiques in his famous treatise on political philosophy, *The Republic,* written four years after the St. Bartholomew Massacre.

We have already noted that French monarchy, which was quite weak at the start of the religious wars, emerged strong as a result of them—so much so that at the end of the century the concentration of power in the person of Louis XIV became absolute. The divine right of kings was a protective countermeasure against the absoluteness of the pope, and as such it was a popular doctrine. It was strengthened by Luther's and Calvin's advocacy of passive obedience to the king and the prince. It was questioned by the French Huguenots, but the necessity of a strong central power to save France from religious disunion blunted the edge of the Huguenot argument. As a matter of fact, France remained Catholic, although the power of the pope was denied in favor of the power of the king.

In Scotland, however, the affairs took a different turn. John Knox modified the Calvinistic injunction of passive obedience. He advocated active opposition to the monarch who is heretical and does not rule according to the moral and just law of God. He is said to have preached that kings do not have power by divine right, but derive their power from the people. It is said that a remark of John Knox to Queen Mary sparked the beginning of democracy in its modern sense. Queen Mary questioned John Knox as to what his status was in the Commonwealth, asking what right he had to question her marriage. He replied that he was a subject of the Commonwealth and a profitable one at that in the sight of God. He was not an earl or a baron and from the queen's point of view may have been quite abject; but that did not bother him a bit. The monarchy in Scotland was Catholic, and unlike the Huguenots, he had more to gain from a policy of resistance than from any other policy. In 1558 he was in exile and under sentence of death, but he was the effective leader of a strong Protestant following. By his policy of resistance he achieved the Scottish Reformation in two years.

In sixteenth-century England, the English Calvinists did not adopt an antiroyalist policy as their French and Scottish counterparts had done. The Anglicans had no special motive for strengthening the doctrine of passive obedience by divine right of kings, although the horrible experience of religious wars may have commended to them passive obedience on utilitarian grounds. In actual fact, the stability and unchallenged power of the Tudor dynasty did not stand in need of invoking the doctrine of the divine right of kings. However, in the seventeenth century when religious war broke out in England, both the defense and refutation of passive obedience were in order. But the situation in England was quite different from that in France. The choice was not beween unity and dismemberment of the nation, but rather between two centers of representative unity: the kings and the Parliament. The necessity of vesting the king with divine right did not arise. As subsequent history shows, Parliament became the effective constitutional agent for national unity, although the kings and queens retained the symbolic significance. It was not the "Leviathan" of Hobbes but the "Second Treatise on Government" of Locke which became the representative document of English political existence, and which in turn had its influence on the American colonies.

PURITAN REVOLUTION

The Puritan revolution is of critical importance for the birth of liberal democracy both in seventeenth-century England and in its American colonies. Charles I was an autocrat who collected taxes without reference to Parliament. In this he was aided and abetted by the Anglican Church. His efforts to impose Anglican liturgy called "Laud's Liturgy" on the Scots led to a rebellion, and he was compelled to turn to Parliament for help. The Puritans in the Parliament used the occasion to attack the king's use of arbitrary powers, unconstitutional prerogatives, and irregular and exorbitant taxes. They regularized the sessions of Parliament, impeached the king's ministers, including Archbishop Laud, and dislodged an episcopal establishment which had supported royal absolutism.

Soon civil war broke out between the king and the troops commanded by Parliament. The king surrendered to the Parliamentary forces in 1646. A plan was drawn up at Westminster to bring the English and Irish churches into a British Reformed Church alongside of Scot Presbyterians. These theocratic Presbyterians lost control in Parliament because of the emergence of left-wing, heretical democratic sects. John Lilburne carried on propaganda among the Puritans of Cromwell's army. Fearing army radicalism, the Parliament disbanded the troops. The troops, however, refused to be disbanded until their rights and liberties were secured. Hence, left-wing democratic Puritanism ousted from Parliament theocratic right-wing Calvinism and a new organization of church and state took place in England.

Similarly, in Massachusetts Bay, Presbyterians and Congregationalists represented an intolerant theocratic republicanism. The seceders drew up "Fundamental Orders of Connecticut" which set aside religious and property requirements for franchise. Still other disaffected members of the Bay Colony set up the commonwealth of Rhode Island under the leadership of Roger Williams. They were governed by a purely civil covenant which was characterized by the word "democratical." This civil, democratic covenant provided for majority rule, government by consent, and due process of law. As one came into a New England town he confronted the church, which also served as the townhouse. Church membership and civic membership were synonymous. Roger Williams distinguished between church and civic society. Alexis de Tocqueville observed later that although church and state were separate, the ethics of the church governed society at large.

The Puritans worked with a small democratic society, the Puritan congregation. This congregation was a fellowship of actively believing members. It was self-governing, composed of people who were all equal in the sight of God. Equality before God was so fundamental that it took precedence over their differences of ability and status. God was equally accessible to all of them for guidance, and they freely took part in discussion regarding the purpose and actions of their little society.

This was a voluntary society and their experience of democracy was not, strictly speaking, political. As a voluntary society they did not use coercion to put their decisions into effect. They persuaded through the medium of discussion. Every member would contribute to the discussion whatever he could, and then all of them together would come to some agreement. As the Quakers said, there would be "the sense of the meeting." Indeed, the Society of Friends was the life-size model of the working of this democratic experience. The Quakers believed that when all members gathered together they enlightened each other, and when people met in the right spirit, something fresh and deep was born out of discussions and silences.

The Puritans experienced the working of democratic behavior, based upon mutual consent and the resolving of their differences through the medium of discussions. It is quite clear that government by consent is a contradiction in terms. Government implies a certain measure of coercion. The fact, however, is that the Puritan experience is based upon a society that governed itself through consent and without the use of violence. It was natural for the

Puritans to see the state after the analogy of the congregation. Government by consent would imply that each and every one should consent to its formation. Actual experience of men tells us that this is an impossible achievement. Since such unanimity is not possible, delegated consent is offered as an alternative. Delegated consent is further interpreted as having a voice in electing, which would imply freedom to vote for or against the makers of law. The democratic argument turns and twists as it tries to justify government based upon consent. Theories of social contract that try to delimit the scope of consent are proposed. The contractual aspects throw into bold relief the freedom of consent, and the freedom of consent raises the question of government by contract.

Democratic theory enshrines the right of free associations within the state. Religious, humanitarian, business, and other free associations can exist in the state although they may have to be regulated. However, the point is constantly made that men form these associations for their own purposes, and their loyalty to them is direct. And it is not taken for granted that in the event of a conflict between the state and a free association that the former will always win.

From voluntary association follows the diversity of opinion and the variety of associations within the uniform body of the state. Therefore the diversity of opinion and the manifold sects have been characteristic features of Anglo-American democracy. The equality of men soon raised the demand for adult suffrage. In the thinking of the Puritans the state had a secondary and instrumental value. Priority was given to voluntary effort, unenforced initiative, and co-operation over against the compulsion of the state. Where voluntary activities fail, there the state is called upon to help—but not to force. The state is to make room for the diversity of spiritual life.

An abiding characteristic of English and American democracy is that it originated in free and voluntary association, and that the state is an imperfect copy of the original true life of the congregation. This is an inheritance from the Puritans.

SECOND TREATISE ON GOVERNMENT

There is really no book that embodies the democratic philosophy of the Puritans, comparable to Hobbes' *Leviathan,* Locke's
Second Treatise on Government, or Rousseau's *Social Contract.*
Their thoughts have to be gleaned from debates, pamphlets, and
other types of literature.

Locke's treatise, which was originally a defense of the Whig
revolution of 1688, had also inspired the democratic thought of
the American colonies. He did not have much to say about the
church. He believed in the reason and good sense of men. Religion
was that to which all good men adhered and their reasonableness
led them to settle their affairs by common agreement. Although
Locke did not share the enthusiasm of the Puritans in religious
matters, his thought in broad outline followed their pattern. He did
not identify state with society. Society was natural to men and they
recognized their mutual interdependence in rights and obligations.
Government was required to take care of criminals and those
others who would jeopardize the normal life of society.

The task of government was to organize enough force to take
care of aggression and at the same time not to permit itself to
become absolute. Like the Puritans, Locke regarded government
as performing an instrumental function and therefore secondary
in status to society. His society was composed of equals who enjoyed equal rights. Government was set up by agreement and consent, and consent was interpreted as abiding by the decision of
majority. Acceptance of the decision of the majority was a require-
ment of practical living. He did not devote much attention to the
tyranny of the majority because he believed that most men were
reasonable and therefore the majority decision would be reasonable also. He was also keenly interested in setting limits to the
power of government. His society was agrarian, where independent, sensible, and resourceful men could support themselves from
the land if they were sufficiently protected from criminals and men
of governmental power at home and aggressors from abroad. The
eighteenth-century American society was of this type. It is easy to

see why the Virginia Declaration of Rights is so much indebted to the theories of John Locke.

The Virginia Declaration of Rights asserts that all men are equally free and independent and have certain inherent rights. When they enter into a state of society they cannot by any compact deprive their posterity of the enjoyment of life and liberty or of the means of acquiring and possessing property and of pursuing and obtaining happiness and safety. All power is derived from and vested in the people, and those who administer power are accountable to them at all times. Government is instituted for the benefit and protection of all the people and for the security of nation and community. That government is the best which is capable of producing the greatest happiness and safety and of safeguarding itself most effectively against maladministration. But when a government is found contrary to these purposes, a majority of the community has an unalienable right to reform, alter, or abolish it by means most conducive to the public warfare.

Elections ought to be free, and all men having sufficient evidence of permanent common interest in and attachment to the community have the right to vote and cannot be taxed or deprived of their property for public uses without their or their representative's consent. Also, they cannot be bound by a law to which they have not given their consent. Without firm adherence to justice, moderation, temperance, frugality, and virtue, and without frequent recourse to basic principles, no free government or the blessing of liberty can be guaranteed to any people. Religion, or the duty we owe to our Creator and the manner in which this duty is discharged, can be directed by reason and conviction and not by force or violence. Therefore all men are free in the exercise of their religion according to the dictates of their conscience, and it is their duty to practice Christian forbearance, love, and charity toward each other.

The Declaration of Independence embodies the same spirit:

> We hold these truths to be self-evident, that all men are created equal, that they are endowed by their Creator with certain unalienable Rights, that among these are Life, Liberty and the pursuit of Happiness; that to secure these rights, Gov-

ernments are instituted among Men, deriving their just powers from the consent of the governed. That whenever any Form of Government becomes destructive of these ends, it is the Right of the People to alter or to abolish it and to institute new Government, laying its foundation on such principles and organizing its powers in such form, as to them shall seem most likely to effect their Safety and Happiness.

These documents assume a self-reliant and resourceful society which is not brought into existence by government. In time of need it is capable of self-organization. It is not a type of society envisaged by Hobbes in his *Leviathan*. It is a society of equals where every man as man has fundamental rights. Both documents emphasize the moral vigor of the people, and since governments tend to assume and prevent power, more emphasis is laid on the restraining rather than on the encouraging of governments. The distinction between government and society is fully emphasized. Thomas Paine wrote that society is formed because of our wants, and its function is to promote happiness. Our wickedness gives rise to government which in turn restrains it. Society is a blessing but government a necessary evil. The more civilized a society is, the less government it requires. It has great powers of self-regulation. William Godwin carried this idea to an extreme and condemned law, punishment, and all compulsory institutions. He felt that reason would convince men that a self-regulating community could be created with the aid of government. The excesses of the French Revolution put an end to this complacent and unrealistic optimism.

THE FRENCH REVOLUTION

The American democracy was a practical realization of the seventeenth-century Puritan ideas. The conditions of the American situation demanded freedom of action, initiative, and resourcefulness. There were new situations and new challenges, and people had to fend for themselves. They did not want any interference from government. The French situation required a strong government to take care of its internal divisions and anarchic conditions. The old social institutions which had a stranglehold on French society could only be shattered by a strong central government. French democracy had to change the society in which it appeared. Minimum government could not do for the French. They, therefore, chose Rousseau over against Locke.

One can say that from England via America the democratic ideas exploded in the French Revolution of 1789. The French National Assembly published a "Declaration of the Rights of Men and Citizens." The Declaration is patterned after the American Declaration. As a matter of fact, the Preamble to the American Declaration and the first two articles of the French are very much alike. For instance, the first two articles read as follows: "(1) Men are born, and always continue, free and equal in respect of their rights. Civil distinctions, therefore, can be founded only in public utility. (2) The end of all political associations is the preservation of the natural and imprescriptible rights of man; and those rights are liberty, property, security and resistance to oppression."

The third article makes the difference between the American and the French forms of democracy. The third article asserts that "The Principle of all sovereignty resides essentially in the nation. No body and no individual can exercise any authority which is not expressly derived from it." This is the point where John Locke takes leave and Jean Jacques Rousseau takes over. The American emphasis is on the limitations of the state power in order to preserve the freedom of the church and other free associations of society. The French emphasize the sovereignty of the nation. Their experience of the church had made them hostile to it. They wanted to deny the hegemony of the church and the pope. Not permitting the distinction between state and society, French democracy took on totalitarian character. The fourth article of the Declaration spells out the totalitarian element by saying, "Law is an expression of the general will. All citizens have the right to concur, either personally or by their representatives, in its formation."

Another characteristic difference between the two systems is their interpretation of the separation of powers. In the American system, the judiciary plays a decisive role. If the executive and legislative branches exceed the limits prescribed for them in the Constitution, the judiciary can pronounce their actions unconstitutional. The Supreme Court is fundamental for the working of American democracy. The French system regards the reviewing actions of the Supreme Court as a transgression of the sovereignty of the Legislature. The French assume that there must be one supreme will in the state and that no limits can be imposed on that will. When all people are permitted either directly or representatively to have a part in the formulation of that will, then the end result will be the general will. This general will can only ordain that which is good for society and forbid that which is harmful. There is, nevertheless, one limitation on the absolute power of national assembly. The people have a right and a duty to insurrection against the despotic violation of the rights of the people.

It must be that practical considerations governing the two national situations have given birth to this profound difference between the two types of democracy. The American system through the device of checks and balances does not permit government to act too hastily. But if it is assumed that the government represents the will of the people, then no limit can be put on its sovereignty.

The French Revolution produced the theory that the enactments of the French General Assembly represent the will of the people; that there is the will of the people called the general will; and that this will is binding on each and every individual. It is clear that Rousseau was a curious mixture of Locke and Hobbes. He believed on the one hand in the moral freedom of individuals, yet on the other hand he took over Hobbes' doctrine of the sovereignty of the nation. According to Hobbes, every individual puts himself completely at the disposal of government. In this sense Rousseau was as absolutist as Hobbes, but in his concept of the general will he somehow included the notion that absolute powers of government were not incompatible with freedom of individuals. It is likely that the general will was the will of the community, which in turn was the will of each individual when that individual was contemplating the general good.

It meant that the general will was the good will of each individual. Consequently, if an individual disagreed with voting which was to express the general will, he was not merely ignorant and misinformed, but positively bad. It is, therefore, reasonable to assume that the idea that "the will of the assembly is the will of the people" is a creation of the French Revolution and cannot be attributed to Rousseau in its entirety. It is not, however, an exaggeration to say that Rousseau perverted democracy in an important sense. His teaching that if a man is in the minority he is selfish leads to the conclusion that minority is wicked and therefore should be suppressed. If judgment is to be passed on men for being in a minority then most men will be tempted to join the majority with less noble aims. The so-called unanimous plebiscites will make mockery of democracy.

These defects are real and harmful, but there is a noble and positive side to the French Revolution. We have already stated that the first practical realization of Puritan ideals was in the American democracy. The French Revolution accorded the ideals of liberty, equality, and fraternity a universal scope. These ideals spoke of men as men everywhere in the world. These democratic ideals were drawn from reason, and reason is common to all men irrespective of historical setting and social inheritance. The universality of these ideals made them attractive in the eyes of all. Democracy in its ideals and purposes became a creed that could be exported to the rest of Europe and indeed to the whole world.

INDUSTRIAL REVOLUTION

The Industrial Revolution cannot be precisely dated as if it happened in 1760. The process was going on before, as it is still going on. It is true that in the latter part of the eighteenth century, invention after invention began to pile up and this led to change in modes of thought and organization of society. Politics and government were deeply affected by it. A new kind of freedom called economic freedom came into existence, and since the problems of society became more complex, efficiency in organization became more prominent. The reconciliation of the natural rights of man with his newly emerging economic rights became a chief problem.

THE UTILITARIANS

The scene shifts to England where in the earlier part of the nineteenth century utilitarians were largely responsible for the development of democratic philosophy. A working alliance arose among evangelical Christianity, the nonreligious radicalism of Jeremy Bentham, and the philosophical radicals. The utilitarians did not form or represent a party. They were a determined band of disciplined and systematic thinkers who shared a common fund of aims and ideals. They had the gift of presenting their views simply and clearly. They exercised an influence—clearly out of proportion to their numbers—on British political thought. They formulated the broad outline of democratic philosophy called political liberalism.

In the interest of spiritual freedom the Puritans had restricted the state. Their views provided room for the diversities of human nature through the formation of voluntary organizations. Like the Puritans, the utilitarians also wanted to safeguard individual freedom. But this freedom was economic freedom. The society having undergone the change from agriculture to industry, there was the demand to have an efficient state to organize the industrial and economic activities of society. Gladstone was right when he said that the basis of political liberalism was rooted in nonconformist religious sects.

On the other hand, the demand for an efficient state was quite different from the minimal government of the Puritans. The utilitarians combined a demand for the efficient state with laissez-faire in economic enterprise. Spiritual freedom and economic freedom have something in common, and if there were common danger they could be effectively united against it. But they do not always and inevitably go together. The utilitarians were influenced by the French materialist philosophers of the eighteenth century. In this political philosophy, and particularly in the economic view of man, they turned to Thomas Hobbes, who was miles apart from the Puritans and John Locke. Hobbes was antireligious but loved science. He applied the model of physics to politics. He believed that man is naturally bad and he needs the power of the Leviathan to keep him away from killing his fellow man. The French materialist philosophers, on the other hand, believed that men's interests were naturally harmonious if they were not abused by priests and kings.

Jeremy Bentham was a thoroughgoing materialist in the tradition of Hobbes. He developed a mechanical view of society. His individuals were like isolated atoms of physics, each self-centered and able to follow consistently its own interests. The mind of man was also like a bundle of ideas. Bentham was extreme in his application of physics to politics, and anything which did not fit in his scientific plan was discarded. He took over from his French teachers the idea of the natural harmony of interests and used it to defend the economic free-enterprise system called laissez-faire. He also retained Hobbes' disharmony of interests, but as a lawyer felt that legal sanctions were necessary to bring about artificial harmony. He, of course, left out the element that men were naturally evil. He did not follow Hobbes in this. His inventive mind tried without success to bring about a synthesis between the efficient mechanism of the state and the free-flowing economic activity. He taught that the greatest good of the greatest number will be served best when an efficient state machinery can be instructed to leave the economic activities of society alone. Utiliarianism helped provide a structure of central and local government to take care of the increasing complexity of industrial society. Also, it helped formulate laws for the conduct of free trade and industry.

The social philosophy of the utilitarians was in fact a program of legal, economic, and political reforms based upon the principle of the greatest happiness of the greatest number. They held this principle to be the rational guide to private conduct and public policy. Their theoretical skill was exercised to make this principle applicable to practical problems, but nobody, including Bentham, achieved any strict systematic form of their various doctrines. John Stuart Mill's criticism was that Bentham's philosophy did not appreciate institutions and their historical growth; also, it worked with a falsely schematic conception of human nature and motives. As a social philosophy, philosophical radicalism had no positive conception of the social good, and its egoistic individualism tended to confirm it at the very time the general welfare of society was beginning to loom large. Its weakness as a political philosophy lay in its negative estimate of government, whereas government was about to assume an increasing part in the general welfare. No sooner had it performed its function than it began to recede in importance.

John Stuart Mill rescued utilitarian ethics from being a mere calculation of pleasures and pains. Human beings should be treated with respect and dignity as bearers of moral responsibility. The utilitarian emphasis in his view lies in the realization of human personality in the actual conditions of a free society. To Mill, political and social freedom was a good in itself because it constituted the very condition of responsible human being. To develop one's own capacities and live one's own life was not a means to happiness but happiness in itself. Liberty was both an individual and a social good. Opinions should not be silenced by violence. A society in which ideas were tested by discussion was the only society which could produce persons capable of enjoying the fruits of open and free discussion. A liberal state in a free society performed a positive function. Legislation should be positive in creating conditions which would make life more humane and civilized.

Thomas Hill Green was indebted to Hegel and yet quite different from him. Hegel represented society as a grouping together of institutions. Institutional treatment of politics and economics was a new discovery and was dealt with in Hegel's philosophy. This was a conspicuous weakness in early liberalism, paying no attention to institutional history. Green's own view that human beings are social implies that organization of society is no more external to them than the organization of their own characters. People discharge their obligations and play their parts in institutions simply because they are personal beings.

According to Green, there is a distinction between society and state. Society is all-inclusive and pluralistic at the same time. It does not require any overarching organization, whereas the state is an organization and therefore not all-inclusive. It is one of the innumerable associations to which people belong, and it enjoys limited power. Even if the state performs regulatory functions it can have an area of privacy for the individual where he can do what he likes on his own responsibility.

The most crucial characteristic of a liberal government is that it not be totalitarian. Majority is to have decent regard for the minority, and the minority is to observe the line between opposition and subversion. No party has permanent tenure. Healthy opposition is necessary in a liberal government and legitimate means should be used to keep a ruling majority out of power. Constitutional institutions are required to enforce this kind of political morality. The community should possess a strong sense of its own purpose and concern for public good and should have some experience in working these institutions.

Alexis de Tocqueville, writing in 1835, was impressed by the vigor of religion in America and baffled by its decline in France. He noted that eighteenth-century philosophers had taught that when knowledge spread and liberty increased, men's hearts and minds would be disaffected in regard to religion. Believing that religion is a natural state of the human mind, he was delighted at the spectacle and strength of Christianity in America, and considered invalid the judgment of the eighteenth-century philosophers. He was, nonetheless, curious to know why Christianity had prospered in America and withered in Europe, particularly in France. He discovered by constant questioning that the basic cause for the strength of Christianity in America was the separation of church and state. He said that the first use the French made of their independence was to attack Christianity. The reason the French did this, he argued, was due principally to the close relation between politics and religion. In Europe, unbelievers attacked Christians as their political rather than religious opponents. Because the Christian religion had been appropriated by a party, they hated it as political belief rather than as religious heresy. People were not anticlerical because the clergy were men of God, but because they were representatives of government.

Alexis de Tocqueville was a Roman Catholic and was naturally interested in the fortunes of Catholics in America, although there were not very many here at that time. He noted that America was inhabited by people who had shaken off the supremacy of the pope and recognized no comparable authority in matters of religion. They brought into the New World a democratic and republican form of Christianity. Later the pope was not avowed as supreme authority and the hierarchic element of Catholic thought was not emphasized, and Catholics could fully take part in the democratic processes and sometimes outdo the democrats. But where the case is different they are subservient and certainly non-democratic.

The Catholic historian Christopher Dawson maintains that the encyclicals of Leo XIII and Pius XI have more kinship with fascism than with liberalism or socialism. Against the right of majorities and the right of free speech, the Roman Catholic Church has consistently maintained the principles of authority and hierarchy. The ruler is not, as he should be in a democratic society, merely a representative of the people; he also has independent authority. Dawson insists that from what he has said a simple identity of fascist and Catholic ideals should not be concluded. It should not be presumed that the Catholics will have no reservations in supporting the fascist program. The fact remains that Catholic hierarchy rests like a rock on the leadership principle with the infallible pope as the supreme head. The pope heads a small political state and a vast spiritual empire. Puritan Protestantism and its offshoots have nourished and supported democracy, not Roman Catholicism.

SECULARIZATION OF CHRISTIANITY

Utilitarianism, by its antireligious attitude and philosophy, secularized Christianity. What the evangelicals called personal religion, the Benthamite liberals called individual energy. Denial of church authority equals indifference to the authority of society and the restraining of state power. Inability to apply principles of growth to religious institutions and historical criticism to the Bible corresponds to Bentham's and his disciples' blindness to see the historical and social context of political and social institutions. More important, the theological emphasis that every man is personally responsible for working out his own salvation was translated into the political principle which treats every individual separately and instructs law to secure freedom for everyone to work out his own happiness.

It is also significant to note that the mission of the church, expressed as it was in the outreach of the church, was gradually transformed into a working-class movement with a definite purpose and program. When, in the eighteenth century, the structured aristocratic Anglican Church would have nothing to do with the successors of the Puritans and in fact rejected the Wesleyans, a division arose in the church. The Anglicans represented the upper classes, and the nonconformists became the champions of the ordinary people. This religious division was good for the development of democracy and democratic institutions. Nonconformity made a substantial religious contribution to the development of democracy in the eighteenth and nineteenth centuries.

Then, starting in the nineteenth and continuing in the twentieth century, the role of religious nonconformity was gradually and then completely taken over by the working-class movement. In the situation of industrial democracy, the trade unions were unlike the guilds of old. In the guilds masters could be members, but the trade unions were entirely composed of the working class, who had to create their own leaders.

Industrial democracy grew up slowly, and small groups of men made many sacrifices for combined action. They practiced rotation of officers and election by lot, and learned to handle the conduct of a referendum. It took time, endurance, experimentation, and disappointments for these little bands of humble, heroic men to organize themselves. By the end of the nineteenth century these trade unions had grown into enormous organizations. The unions became fighting organizations and were recognized by the employers as well as by the state. Men of position and education, who under ordinary circumstances would have been the leaders, have been left out from the beginning, and in a real sense industrial democracy has been the result of a working-class movement. Industrialism has given rise to the working-class movement, and this movement has made its effective contribution to democracy, although it does imply that Christianity has been secularized in the European and American scene. In Japan and India it has had the effect of secularizing religion and democratizing industrial human relations.

From the religious wars of the sixteenth and seventeenth centuries to the technological twentieth century, there has been an accelerated primacy of the political, economic, and technical over the religious and clerical. Modern liberal democracy, although inspired by Protestant evangelical Christianity, has in the course of time drastically secularized it. About democratic utilitarianism it is said that although it was the Anglo-American version of atheism and was deliberately antireligious, it was still able to co-operate and join forces with Protestant revival in its emphasis upon individualism, humanitarianism, and austere self-discipline.

5

Communism, Christianity, Democracy

The broad historical context in which the interrelations of communism, Christianity, and democracy have taken place in the past has already been described in general terms. It is necessary to constitute the present theater of events to show continuity or discontinuity with the past. Two documents spell out the scope of present and future encounter.

The first document consists of reports of the Central Committee to the Twentieth and Twenty-First Congresses of the Communist Party, submitted by Nikita S. Khrushchev in 1956 and 1958 respectively. Both of these far-reaching reports assume as their basis the classical doctrines and programs of Marxism-Leninism.

The second document is entitled "Goals for Americans," and is a report of the President's Commission on National Goals published in 1960. This modern enunciation of American goals and programs of action is set forth within the scope of the Declaration of Independence drafted by Thomas Jefferson and adopted by the Continental Congress on July 4, 1776.

The historic East-West embraces and departures, emulations and conflicts are continued, and their implications are portrayed for the present and the future. The present and the future of Christianity are involved in these encounters, as was its past. Let us see in brief what these documents have to say.

The Twentieth Congress of the Communist Party convened

only three years and four months after the Nineteenth Congress, and
Khrushchev presented his report with a sense of historical urgency
which had profound bearing for the programs of the Communist
Party and the strength of the Soviet Union relative to the Western
world, particularly to the U.S.A.

INDUSTRIAL GROWTH

Khrushchev gives figures of the industrial growth of the
U.S.S.R. from 1929 to 1955. In twenty-six years the Soviet
Union increased its industrial growth twentyfold, in spite of the
war damage to its national economy. This measure of growth is a
sign of competitive strength of socialism in relation to capitalism.
The U.S.S.R. holds second place in industrial output of pig iron,
steel, aluminum, copper, machinery, electricity, cement, and coal.
The Soviet Union is ahead of France, West Germany, and Britain.
Khrushchev stresses the fact that his country is steadily catching
up with the United States.

According to him, the Soviet Union and other socialist countries are developing peacefully and in an all-around manner. Emphasis is laid on heavy industry which is foundational, but agriculture and light industries are not ignored. The standard of living is
rising steadily and culture is flourishing. He is thrilled by the pros-
pects of harnessing atomic energy and by other achievements of
modern science for developing the land, mineral, and water resources of the country in such a way that there will be an abun-
dance of food and consumer goods.

By following the lines laid down by the great Lenin, the Communist Party has ensured the development of heavy industry upon
which all other industries are based. He promises that Lenin's
policy will be followed consistently and firmly by the party. He
gives figures to support the fact that the engineering industry has
made the most rapid progress during the fifth Five-Year Plan.
He says that the socialist system of economy permits them to make
rapid progress in industrial production, which is not the case with
capitalism. He cites the fact that during the fifth Five-Year Plan
the rate of Soviet industrial output was three times as high as that
of the U.S.A. and 3.8 times higher than that of Britain. He gives

percentages of per capita output for the fifth plan. Pig iron increased by 60%, steel by 52%, coal by 37%, oil by 72%, electric power by 71%, cotton fabrics by 40%, woolen fabrics by 48%, and sugar by 24%. He confessed that this rate of per capita growth still lagged behind the leading capitalists countries. Much effort is required to fulfill the basic economic task, which is to catch up with and surpass the most developed capitalist country in the world.

Capital investment increased to 94% as compared with the fourth plan. The construction of electric power stations went up 3.4 times. The quality and quantity of production increased. And when he said that in doing all this the Soviet Union took a new major step forward in its gradual march from socialism to communism, there was prolonged applause.

The sixth Five-Year Plan has a greater potential of growth, and the Central Committee of the Communist Party has addressed itself to the task of increased industrial production and has introduced new measures. Why has the committee done so? Because the industrial successes made the business executives and party workers complacent and conceited, answers Khrushchev. The party had to be mobilized in order to overcome this lag in industry. The directives of the sixth plan are sweeping and comprehensive. Under these draft directives, industrial production was to rise in 1960 about 65% of the level of 1955. Similarly, the means of production and consumer goods were to rise 70% and 60% respectively. In this way, at the end of the sixth plan the industrial output in the U.S.S.R. will be more than five times the prewar 1940 level.

After having said that, Khrushchev lectured on the relative merits of capitalist and socialist production. The aim of capitalist production is the extraction of bigger profits. This is done by the exploitation of workers and the expansion of production. But the expansion of production comes into conflict with the decline of demand and consumption which he says is inevitable under capitalism. Capitalism suffers from a deep contradiction between production and consumption which it is unable to overcome.

Socialism, however, has overcome this contradiction. Socialism aims at the satisfaction of the growing needs of the working people or of the society as a whole. The expansion of heavy industry leads to the accelerated development of industries directly related to the fulfilling of the needs of the people. Since powerful heavy industry has been developed, attention will be concentrated on the means of production and consumer goods. Khrushchev gave a solemn promise that the needs and the requirements of the Soviet people will have first priority, and that the Communist Party considers this its prime duty.

AGRICULTURE

Alongside of a strong industry, there should be a highly developed agriculture capable of producing foodstuffs and other necessary materials for the needs of the people and the demands of the state. The growth and development of socialist economy and labor productivity and the reduction of retail prices has increased the purchasing power of workers and collective farmers.

The increase in the purchasing power raised before the party a question of national significance, i.e., how to increase the farm products. The Central Committee of the party, meeting in plenary sessions, brought out into the open serious mistakes in the management of agriculture. It therefore laid out a comprehensive program for the increase of farm products. During 1954 and 1955 capital investment in agriculture amounted to 34,400 million rubles, which is 38% more than the total investment in agriculture during the fourth plan. A great many tractors and other types of machinery were made available. The collective farms were given substantial incentives because the procurement prices of farm products were considerably raised. This added 20,000 million rubles to the collective farms in these two years. The Machine Tractor Stations have been transformed into model socialist establishments, and thousands of engineers, technicians, and party workers have gone to work at the Machine Tractor Stations and at collective and state farms.

Data shows that more labor is used to produce a ton of milk or meat in the U.S.S.R. than in the U.S.A. Competitively speaking, more people are employed in agriculture in the Soviet Union than in the U.S.A. Khrushchev, then, says that the American example cannot be followed blindly because the motive there is profit-making. He claims that from 1940 to 1954 about 1,300,000 farmers were ruined in the United States. The big farmer is a capitalist and regards labor as a source of profit. The capitalist throws a laborer out if his health is poor and he cannot produce the required labor.

In contrast, he maintains, things are different in the U.S.S.R. because, the collective farms being co-operative enterprise, the farmers are owners. In a socialist society everything is so arranged that the requirements of men are met. If one of the collective farmers cannot, for reasons of health, work at full capacity, he is not turned out. In spite of the difference in outlook, it is still the case, he admits, that the U.S.S.R. employs more agricultural labor than is necessary. There the agricultural planning should be looked into critically, and anything that can be learned from foreign experience should be used. It is certain, assures Khrushchev, that the Soviet people led by the Communist Party will perform this task.

RISE IN MATERIAL AND CULTURAL STANDARDS

The standard of living of the Soviet people has risen because of the advance in industry and agriculture. During the fifth plan the national income of the U.S.S.R. rose by 68%, and Khrushchev reminded his audience that three-fourths of that income goes to satisfy the personal needs of the Soviet people. In the same period, the state spent 689,000 million rubles for social insurance, paid holidays for all types of workers, medical services, pensions, and other amenities of that kind. About 90% more consumer goods were sold to the people in 1955 than in 1950. The food, clothing, and cultural needs of the people are better supplied than before. One indication of the material well-being is an increase of about 16 million in population during the fifth plan. The Draft Directives of the sixth Five-Year Plan are designed to raise the wages of the workers by 30% and collective farmers' incomes by 40%. Khrushchev proposed a five-day working week with eight hours of work a day and two days free. Housing is to be increased and improved to take care of the growing population and of the movement of people from the country to the big cities. Many things still remain to be done for the welfare of the people, and it is the welfare of the people on which the attention of the Communist Party and the Soviet Government is focused.

In April of 1958, the Communist Party put into effect a scheme of Khrushchev's, which would encourage those collective farms which can purchase and maintain their own machinery such as tractors, combines, and other mechanical implements. This was to increase efficiency and eliminate waste from agricultural production. *Pravda* had justified this plan as a means of overtaking the United States in the production of meat, milk, and butter. In June of the same year it was announced that compulsory deliveries of agricultural products from the collective farms to the state should be in the form of purchases, although still based on the quota system of production. The introduction of these measures seems to show that the realities of supply and demand, profit and loss, and cost and price are more potent incentives than ideology.

In November of 1958, the Central Committee of the Soviet Communist Party introduced, for discussion and later for presentation to the Twenty-First Congress, a Seven-Year Plan instead of the Five-Year one. The 1959-65 plan visualized that gross industrial products will increase by 80%, consumer goods by 65%, agricultural products by 70%. In addition, a vast housing program is proposed and 40% increase in real income is promised. Khrushchev gives the evaluation of the Seven-Year Plan in the following manner:

> Comrades, the Seven-Year Plan will exert a deep influence on the international situation and will be a new triumph for Marxism-Leninism. Our successes in fulfilling the plan will attract millions of new adherents to the side of socialism, will lead to the strengthening of the forces of peace and weakening of the forces of war, and will cause tremendous changes, not only in our own country, but throughout the world; there will be a decisive shift in favor of socialism in the economic sphere of the world arena.
>
> The economy is the chief field in which the peaceful competition between socialism and capitalism is unfolding, and we are interested in winning this competition in an historically short period.

If the goals and targets for 1965 and 1970 are realized as planned, it will constitute a major and frightening challenge to the West for the allegiance of Asia, Africa, and Latin America. Ac-

cording to the plan, the Communist bloc will outproduce the rest
of the world, and the Soviet Union will have significantly reduced
the United States' lead over it. The Soviet people will have
more of everything for themselves in the form of heavy industry, homes, food, and television sets. By 1970 the people of the
Soviet Union will have the highest standard of living and will be
outproducing the United States on an absolute as well as a per
capita basis.

This is indeed a bold, ambitious, and competitive plan. It will
be helpful to see the assets and liabilities of this grand design. The
mineral wealth of the Soviet Union is well in excess of that of the
United States. It has highly developed technology and is therefore
capable of expanding its industrial base. The Soviet population is
not given to strikes and production layoffs. Moreover, being relatively better educated now than before, it can be more productive.
The Soviet economy, being centrally controlled, is not subject to
economic recessions in the manner in which a free economy is
susceptible. Agricultural reforms which eliminate inefficiency and
waste have been introduced and the production capacities of the
people have been raised.

On the side of liabilities, it can be said that to realize the
proposed production targets, an enormous capital investment will
be required for new factories, mines, and communication systems.
This will also compete with Khrushchev's commitments on housing, short hours of work, and consumer goods. Many of the new
finds in raw materials lie in thinly populated areas and require
transportation of populations. How this can be accomplished without force and without antagonizing the people remains to be seen.
Some of the capital Khrushchev plans to raise by lowering farm
prices as a result of efficiency in agricultural production, which is
supposed to lower production costs. But the point is whether or
not the Soviet farmer will accept reduction in prices. Khrushchev
also presupposes for his ambitious plans a stability in the international sphere. There is no assurance that tensions in international
relations will not require further expenditure on military preparedness, nor is it certain that there will not be another rebellion of the
Hungarian or Polish type.

Soviet economy faces enormous hurdles, and it is doubtful whether or not targets set can be realized on schedule. However, if Soviet economic and technological progress continues and this is accompanied by any serious economic recession in the West, the effect on the underdeveloped countries will be simply disastrous. An ascending scale of Soviet standard of living will increase the appeal of communism not only for the less developed countries, but also for the poorer countries of Europe, such as Italy. The West will also face the problem of increased Communist military strength because of a substantial output of steel and other basic materials. Business competition will acquire a new tempo because there will be keen competition for markets and extension of trade.

Soviet communism has acquired such a measure of confidence that it has embarked upon a competitive struggle with the West on the broad spectrum of political, economic, technological, and cultural life. The implications of the Khrushchev reports will unfold in the course of time. It is quite clear that the lines of Russian and Soviet history converge in the attempt to catch up with the West and then to surpass it. This is a historic struggle. It has a long past; it fills the present and will continue for an indeterminate future. The Khrushchev reports are aimed particularly at the United States of America. It is the U.S.A. that Khrushchev wants desperately to catch up with and surpass. He makes full use of ideology to declare that history and time are on his side. He uses strategy and tactics to the hilt to shorten the period and distance of his desired victory. What is the response of the American nation and society to this Russian-Soviet challenge?

GOALS FOR AMERICANS

The American response is presented by way of a report to the President entitled "Goals for Americans." President Eisenhower appointed a nonpartisan commission to restate American goals and programs for the decade of the sixties. The original basis for American goals is the Declaration of Independence. The report to the President vindicates the mighty vision of the Declaration for the decade of the sixties. This not only meets the Communist challenge but also brings up to date the heritage of the past.

THE INDIVIDUAL

The central concern of the report, as of the Declaration, is the individual. Political, social, and economic institutions of the nation serve to enhance the dignity and promote the highest development of the citizen. A wide choice of opportunities is created for the responsible exercise of freedom by the individual citizen. From the concern for the individual springs equal treatment for men and women. The range of their incentives is enlarged so that self-development and self-expression may increase and mature. Political and economic power is widely distributed for the purpose of creating a wide range of free choice in vocations and occupations. Education and science foster a spirit of free inquiry and exchange. One man respects the freedom of the other, and the love of liberty does not impose its will upon others to create a spirit of bondage and conformity. Ideas and individuals are not rejected because they are controversial. Unity is not to be confused with unanimity, and the right to dissent is undeniable.

EQUALITY

During this decade discrimination on the basis of religion, sex, and particularly race must be eliminated with great speed. Racial prejudice is morally wrong. It is dangerous and economically wasteful. The status of women has undergone a radical change and rapid progress has been made in the realization of equality. However, respect for the rights of an individual means every individual. He is to enjoy equality in voting, holding office, promotion in status upon qualification, and acquisition of jobs. He should have equal opportunity to buy a home and to participate in community affairs. The basic responsibility in bringing about changes in prejudicial habits lies with individuals. The government has the responsibility to stimulate attitudinal changes. The report recommends that by 1970 discrimination in higher education should be eliminated, and in publicly supported schools rapid progress must be made by every state.

THE DEMOCRATIC PROCESS

The test of every nation is the actual liberty its people enjoy. The practice of democracy is the only device by which such a test can be met. The goal of this decade and the succeeding ones is to ensure the preservation and perfection of the democratic process in the United States. For the working of the democratic process, the individual citizen must act responsibly, form reasoned opinions regarding matters of public policy, and participate in the civic process of choosing public representatives. The organs of the Federal Government should be improved in the light of circumstances, and Congress should evaluate its procedures when events present new evidence. The democratic process can work best when the public is well informed. The mass media should improve the quality of information. The American people are well informed but their sources of information should continually be enriched to deal with complex problems. The Federal Government should have in its employ persons of competence and imagination comparable to those in private business and professions.

At the local level, means must be found to co-ordinate numerous local governments for the solution of common problems. Power to solve problems of local governments should be shared instead of having these problems continue to be solved separately and inadequately.

EDUCATION

For the health and the strength of the individual and the nation, education should be provided at every level and in every discipline. The teaching techniques should be brought up to date. The increase in population will demand augmentation in the content and facilities of education. The complexity of the demands of a changing world situation add urgency to the educational task. Greater resources should be made available at all levels and a greater proportion of the gross national product should be devoted to education. This increase of resources would be beneficial to the individual, to the democratic process, and to the posture of the nation in the world.

In some states of the Union, four-fifths of the students finish high school and one-half go on to an institution of higher learning. But there are other states where the picture is not so good. There are states where less than one-half of the students finish high school and not even twenty percent enter college. The goal for the decade of the sixties is to see that two-thirds of the students complete their high school education and one-third of them go on to college. By 1970 financial support for education from private and public sources should be about $40 billion, which is double that of 1960. The role of the Federal Government should be expanded to account for $33 billion by 1970. Education is, of course, primarily the responsibility of the states. Authority is delegated to local bodies for public education at the elementary and secondary levels.

The report recommends that in scientific education more resources should be allotted to the pursuit of basic research in order to extend further the understanding of the world. Applied science and technology should be vigorously pursued because of their benefits for the betterment of health, economic development, and military power. At this juncture in history high priority should be given to science and technology for military purposes. However, concentration on these is not for the purpose of remaining ahead of any nation, but because in the long run their pursuit is in keeping with American tradition. Space programs should be chosen selectively, not for spectacular effect, but for sound accomplishment. Nationalistic competition should not drive us to the adoption of extravagant programs which would divert our resources in men and material. Students capable of receiving specialized scientific education should be given the best education that our scientific pool of talent can devise, and this education should be made available as early as possible. Highly trained people should not be employed in jobs which do not challenge their highest ability and training.

A national life will not be well rounded unless the humanities, social sciences, and natural sciences are allowed to make their full contributions. History, literature, psychology, and economics help the individual feel, understand, and communicate. These avenues of knowledge offer sensitive human values. The teaching and learning of foreign languages provide the knowledge of other people and cultures and also help in the performance of international diplomatic tasks. Succeeding generations will judge the United States as a civilized and humane nation by the creative activities of its citizens in art, architecture, music, literature, and the sciences. Richer cultural enjoyment and fulfillment should be encouraged. The theater must have wide community support; it should be stimulated in colleges and universities and should be nationally rehabilitated. Thus far, television has not fully appropriated its own educational and cultural capabilities.

THE DEMOCRATIC ECONOMY

The report emphasizes the compatibility of the economic system with the political system. Economic power, therefore, should be diffused rather than concentrated. In order to maintain fair competition, overconcentration of economic power in corporations, unions, and other organizations should be carefully watched. Citizens should have a wider range of choice of jobs, goods, and services. Government's participation should be limited to the protection of national interest or to those areas in which the private resources cannot meet the demands. Government must continue to exercise its regulatory powers for the protection of investor and consumer interests. It must continue to administer antitrust laws and must carefully watch cases of collusion and conflict of interest. Collective bargaining between workers and employers should continue as the main means of settlement of wages and working conditions. Conferences among management, union leaders, and public representative should be held to learn each other's problems and the problems facing the economy as a whole. The influence of corporations and unions on the private life of their members should be restricted. There should be a greater employment of women and older workers. Especially unmarried women and women whose children have grown and left the home can use their abilities gainfully in paid or voluntary employment. The report suggests that this pool of talent may be the one that is inadequately used.

The growth of the economy should continue to be based on the free enterprise principle. The growth should be as little subject to inflationary pressures as possible. Investment at an increased rate in the public sector is quite consistent with the principle of growth. In the decade of the sixties there will be an increase of 13,500,000 in the work force. The growth of the economy is essential to provide for the additional jobs. The report recommends overhaul of the tax structure, including depreciation allowances. This will create fresh climate for new investment. Investment and consumption should be balanced. New ventures involving risk and growth potential should be encouraged. Education at all levels should aim at creating a working force at once more efficient and more flexible.

Competition with the Communist countries is not desirable for the sake of competition. The measure of economic growth lies in our capacity to fulfill our needs of defense, education, health, and foreign aid. Technological changes should be introduced to strengthen the economy, but their introduction should constantly bear in mind the health and well-being of individuals. Unemployment through technological change should be balanced by retraining of workers and creation of new jobs. A combination of engineering and management talent should be encouraged to take care of increasingly complex technology. By imaginative and skilled management new weapons should be brought to operational use in less time. The weapon systems are so costly and complex that saving of time becomes the critical factor. There should not be inter-service wrangling on specially sponsored weapon systems.

AGRICULTURE

Agriculture does not bring to the farmer a competitive return in relation to the rest of the economy. The technological change has already made its impact on agriculture. In the decade of the fifties, agricultural productivity rose three times as fast as the economy as a whole. This means that more people and resources are committed to agriculture than the foreign and domestic needs of the country would justify. Farmers are leaving agriculture; in the ten years from 1950 to 1960 agricultural population was reduced by one million families. There is, however, another problem which concerns 50% of the farmers, whose farm output is only

10% and who operate at subsistence level. Nonfarm jobs have to be found for over a million farm operators whose present yearly income is less than $1500. Government subsidies and farm supports have to be maintained in order to ease the shock of transition caused by the introduction of technological change.

LIVING CONDITIONS

Slums should be cleared and decay in big cities should be stopped. Minority and low-income groups should be helped so that they do not concentrate in big cities. Suburbs should not be allowed to grow in a haphazard way. The cost of public services should be shared by cities and suburbs on an equitable basis. Regional planning should be encouraged so that urban centers of population will have their own industries and institutions of education, culture, and recreation. The populations of these urban centers should be balanced in backgrounds and spread of income levels. Parks and recreational facilities for a growing population should be adequately arranged. Racial discrimination in housing should be eliminated. Federal assistance should be withheld where discrimination is practiced. Federal support should be given for housing programs of moderate cost. Services to slum areas are as important as the clearance of slums.

For adequate maintenance of the health and welfare of the people, there should be more hospitals, nurses, and nursing homes. Government should continue to subsidize the building of hospitals, the cost of medical expenditure should be reduced, medical insurance should be further extended, and scholarships should be provided through medical schools and during the period of internship. The need for doctors is great, but enrollment in medical schools has been declining. Places in medical schools should be increased, and able students of modest means should be helped to enroll in them. Seventeen million people suffer from mental illness, costing the state governments about a billion dollars a year. More facilities and continued research in the problems of mental health are required to meet the problem. Sustained research should be continued to learn more about the causes of family breakdown, and methods should be developed to prevent juvenile delinquency.

FOREIGN RELATIONS

The primary aim of the United States' foreign policy should be the continued preservation of its own independence and of the freedom of its institutions. The nation's international posture should be neither offensive nor defensive, but balanced and self-confident. The United States should always be ready to co-operate with nations of similar interests and ideals, should work steadfastly to ease international tensions, and should search tirelessly for honorable ways to come to an understanding with opponents. It should press for the reduction in armaments, with safeguards. Freedom versus totalitarianism is the issue of our times. The United States, along with other free nations, should not permit the subversion of nationalism into Communist totalitarianism. Free nations working together can influence the choice in favor of freedom by helping to encourage political and economic stability based upon progress and justice. American goals abroad are part and parcel of goals at home. Americans must endeavor to build an open and peaceful world by making democracy work and by seeing to it that the life of the individual is more free and fruitful.

World economy will be healthy when world trade is free. It should be an American goal to help make the world free for trade. The United States should join other free nations to arrange for the lowering of international tariffs and restrictions of quotas. This should be done in keeping with the health and the integrity of national economy. The practices of the totalitarian governments should be resisted and effectively countered. It is natural for the less developed countries to protect their young industries against foreign competition. The United States in its earlier days had to do the same.

Nevertheless, the United States should work for the lowering of trade barriers in other parts of the world, and particularly in the large regional trading groups. Export trade must be conducted with greater imagination and energy. The adverse balance of payments is not due to foreign trade policy; there are other factors which of necessity have entered in. In order to rectify this unfavorable balance of payments, export trade has to be intensified. Other industrially developed nations should join with the United States in helping the underdeveloped countries of the world. Also, the allies should bear an equitable burden for the defense of the free world.

THE LESS DEVELOPED NATIONS

American ideals inspire the American people to come to the help of young and free nations. In order to foster national freedom and the growth of free institutions in these countries, it is necessary that the other developed free nations of the world join the United States in programs of foreign aid. Institutions such as the World Bank should be supported for the loan of development funds. The report estimates that by investing $20 billion, three-fourths of which comes from their own savings, these developing countries are increasing their production by 2%. But the increase of population eats this up, showing little or no growth in the standard of living. However, it is reasonable to assume that their economic growth can be doubled in five years, if the foreign investment can be increased from its present $5 billion to $9 billion by 1965. Such an increase would imply about one percent of the Western developed nations' combined gross national product. The United States would be contributing $5 to $5½ billion per year by 1965. The relationship of the United States to Latin America is special, and calls for a close co-operation on the basis of partnership. A large number of qualified Americans should be encouraged to live and work abroad. Already more than half a million are employed in private and government employment, but their number must increase during this decade in order to raise the level of exports and foreign investments and to carry on the programs of economic and technical assistance.

DEFENSE OF THE FREE WORLD

Communist designs and actual aggression and subversion are a constant threat to the life and liberty of free nations. To safeguard freedom and democracy at home and abroad requires not only vigilance but also powerful countermeasures. In this decade the Communist expansion must be contained and the area of liberty and democratic choice should be extended throughout the world.

We must have an ever ready military capability to act as deterrent. We should be ready and willing to make necessary sacrifices for this purpose. The hostility of Communist China to the U.S.A. makes it necessary for Pacific defenses to be strengthened and for the ties with the Pacific allies to be reinforced. Communist China is going to be more aggressive and hostile during this decade than the U.S.S.R. Already its strong conventional forces exert a considerable impact on Asia, and if it develops atomic capability its threatening power will become enormous. We should continue the support of the Republics of Korea and China, help strengthen Japan, and give military and economic aid to the countries of southeast Asia. Our own military preparedness should be kept on the alert, and a country like India should be given major economic assistance for its development. Our military alliances in Asia, the Middle East, and Europe should be strengthened and the Organization of American States should receive our unstinting support. We should hope and work for the day when the Communist-dominated people will be able to exercise the right of self-determination.

Nuclear war will be a world tragedy from which no one can gain anything. Our aim, therefore, should be disarmament, but this will remain a distant goal unless the sources of distrust and fear among people are eliminated. Control of nuclear weapons can only be a step-by-step process with attendant international inspection. Since the control of nuclear weapons has a direct bearing on national security, an extended analysis of political, military, and technical issues should be made to become the basis for negotiation and policy formulation. The support of the United Nations is one of the major foreign policy aims of the United States. It is the only worldwide instrument for the building of a community of nations. It will be under maximum stress during this decade, and will require the wholehearted support of the United States.

After stating American goals at home and abroad, the report contains the following sentences in its concluding remark: "The very deepest goals for the Americans relate to the spiritual health of our people. The right of every individual to seek God and the well-springs of truth, each in his own way, is infinitely precious.

We must continue to guarantee it, and we must exercise it, for ours
is a spiritually based society. Our material achievements in fact
represent a triumph of the spirit of man in the mastery of his
material environment."

PLURALIZATION IN THE PRESENT EAST-WEST CONTEXT

Pluralization has occurred within the sphere of communism as
well as in Western democracy. The behavior of France within the
Western family of nations and the acute form of the Sino-Soviet
conflict mirror this pluralization. American-French relations indi-
cate that General De Gaulle believes that the postwar period has
ended, and therefore the alliance necessitated by World War II
should be shaken up to deal with new historical trends and realities.
The recognition of Communist China is a result of this attitude.
National aspiration and goals have also come to the forefront.
Strengthened by the conviction that the threat of nuclear war has
receded, France wants to become a full-fledged nuclear power in
order to play her historic role not only in Europe but in the world
at large. Whereas France is an extreme case, other Western nations
are also working for the loosening of the alliance in pursuit of
national interest. This raises serious questions for the national and
world position of the United States. She is still the de facto pillar
for the peace and hence the prosperity of western Europe, although west European countries act as though that is not the case.
A drastic reappraisal of her own role is quite in order for the
U.S.A.

The Communist monolithic unity has been eroded gradually.
Although Stalin is the one who initiated this movement by his
doctrine of socialism in one country, outwardly it can be dated in
1948 when Yugoslavia was evicted from the Communist household. The process of Communist pluralization is rooted in nationalism. The demands and needs of different Communist nations are
divergent and various. They cannot gear their national economies
to the needs and demands of the U.S.S.R. To take care of the
peculiar national needs requires the modification of Communist
universal ideology.

The heresy of revisionism is born in the hardheaded pursuit of

national interest. The result of the revisionist heresy is that Soviet
Russia is not considered the only authoritative interpreter of Communist doctrine and practice. Revisionism also gives Communist
nations the excuse to be free from the political and economic
domination of Moscow. The tables have been turned on the
U.S.S.R. by Communist China through the accusation of the
heresy of revisionism. Communist China claims that she is orthodox, and accuses the Soviet Union of having become heterodox. In
fact, through this device Communist China wants to claim leadership of the Communist world. With the stakes so high, the Soviet
Union has drawn closer to Yugoslavia, both as fact and symbol,
and has become relatively open to the West. There is real trouble
in the household of communism, but relative openness to the West
augurs well for a somewhat hopeful prospect for world peace and
order.

THE SECULARIZATION OF CHRISTIANITY
(*Christianity and Communism*)

In studying the relationship of Christianity and communism on
the one hand and Christianity and democracy on the other, we
have noted one conspicuous feature—the secularization of Christianity. Christianity makes total claims on the life of man. It develops a world outlook on the affairs of life. Marxism-Leninism keeps
the idea of a universal viewpoint but changes its substance. It is
totalitarian and makes total claims in the name of a binding ideology. Atheism is its "god" and it calls for sacrifices in its name.

Nicholas Berdyaev makes a profound observation when he says
that the teaching and preaching of atheism are designed to deny
everything Christian, but communism does not realize that the
habit and capacity of making sacrifices has been taught by Christianity. Natural man is not given to making sacrifices, so although
communism denies Christianity, it cannot help but presuppose
something of it when it calls upon adherents to make sacrifices for
an idea. The dictatorship of the proletariat headed by the party is
the church militant. The working of the dialectic is comparable to
the working of Providence. The Kingdom of God is that state of
communism which transcends socialism. The holy scriptures of

communism are the Marxist-Leninist writings. Just as rules of interpretation are applied to the biblical text, so also the works of Marx and Lenin are exegeted to explain historical events. The mission of Christianity has been changed into the mission to convert the world in line with Communist objectives. The substance of the Christian message has been changed in much the same way as Marx tried to change the teachings of Hegel. The fact, however, remains that in spite of persistent and single-minded efforts to eradicate Christianity in Russia and other Communist countries, it has survived and shows no signs of dying.

In the Soviet Union, from its very inception, the only rival to communism has been Russian Orthodox Christianity. Although there are other forms of religion, such as Islam, Judaism, and Buddhism, the main confrontation has been between communism and Christianity, and the latter has managed to survive and to keep some of its institutional forms. Smaller Christian denominations sometimes give out statistics, but it is difficult to measure the strength of religion through numbers. It is worth noting that between ardent religious beliefs and militant atheism there are many degrees of belief and unbelief. There is a sizable group of people who subscribe neither to religion nor irreligion. And, of course, this is not peculiar to Russia; they are present in every society.

Russian Orthodoxy and other religions have not been eradicated. The fact is that atheistic propaganda has not been altogether successful because the Communists have not been able to create a new civilization and a new man to bury religion for good. People did not join the Communist movement for merely antireligious reasons. They had mixed reasons, some idealistic and others opportunistic. Even Lenin, who fully subscribed to Marx's dictum that religion is the opiate of the people, did not hesitate to recruit religious believers in the working class as long as they did not oppose party program.

It was only in 1929 and 1930 when party purges took place that those with religious affiliation were expelled. In the purge of 1933 it was discovered that in Moldavia certain members of the Communist Party not only were practicing Christians, but were even collecting money for the repair of churches. It is said they went to the purge commission singing Christian hymns on their way. Again in 1954 it was by chance that a scientist belonging to the Leningrad Academy of Medical Sciences was discovered to be a secret believer while having been a member of the Communist Party for twelve years.

This discloses the presence of hidden Christians among the Communists just as there are secret Communists among the ranks of the Christians. The League of Militant Godless was disbanded when the hordes of Hitler crossed the frontiers of Russia and the atheistic government was in desperate need of the help of believers. If Christianity had disappeared from the Soviet scene, then the Marxist theory that religion is a bourgeois phenomenon would have been proved true. But since it is present in the society which claims to be classless, it has to be explained in its own terms.

Christianity is not an alien but an internal phenomenon. There are three groups of workers in the Soviet Union: the industrial proletariat or workers, collective farmers, and the "toiling intelligentsia." The collective farmers include the largest number of believers, and the "toiling intelligentsia" the least, especially those who are in the higher income group, while the industrial workers fall in between. During periods of excessive drought, the collective farmers expressed their religious enthusiasm by forming processions praying for rain and good harvest. Such processions were carried out not only in the prewar period but also after World War II.

It is reported that after Stalin's death there were pleas to make him an eternal member of some Soviet body. The idea was to immortalize him and permit a cult of adoration to grow around him. The successors of Stalin did not allow it, and as a result there was a spirit of demoralization among the young people who had grown up in awe of him. There was a mood of nihilism—which in the Soviet Union ranges from disruptive hooliganism to the celebration of religious values. If the young, even a fraction of them, suffer from a vacuum which requires idealistic or religious filling, it is a judgment on the ineffectiveness of Communist teaching and propaganda.

Another group which remains somewhat unaffected by the

antireligious propaganda is the women of the Soviet Union. According to those who engage in antireligious propaganda, about 70% of the believers are women, and in some cases their proportion runs as high as 80% or 90%.

Communist theorists speculate that when the Communist revolution is complete on a world scale, religion will disappear. They argue that at present foreign religious influences are operative in the Soviet Union. There is some truth in this; when in a progressive and industrial society Christianity is respected, it baffles the Communists who think technology should have done away with religion, but it encourages the believers in their difficult situation.

Christianity has had a long history in Russia. It has passed through difficult times. In order to hold on to its substance it has made many sacrifices and adjustments. There are many hurdles before it in the Soviet Union. It is like a depressed class in a supposedly classless society, but it has survived and has a future. For communism to maintain this invidious class distinction is to defeat the claims of its own ideology.

Since Christianity has not been eliminated from the Soviet scene, there are only two alternatives left. One is to launch a reinforced attack on Orthodox Christianity and other forms of religion in order to eliminate them completely. Past history and present national, intra-Communist, and international circumstances would make such a course of action extremely inadvisable. The other course of action is to permit atheism to become a matter of personal belief. To do this is not to help religion but to save the classless character of Soviet ideology.

Marx and Lenin both knew the social significance of Christianity and religion in general. They took this point very seriously, and wanted to eliminate Christianity as a competitor of the Communist way of life. Lenin, however, advised Communists operating in the Western countries to emphasize that Christianity is a personal affair of the individual and should not be permitted to interfere with social issues.

Could it be that the day has come when "atheism" as the religion of the Communists may become a personal and individual affair quite distinct from their politics and economics? Should this occur in any significant degree, then communism would be dented as a total world view with "religious" sanctions and would become a political and economic philosophy and method. Its test would then lie not as an ideology which fills the religious vacuum, but as a philosophy and method of achieving what it promises. It would be the pragmatic test which would decide its ultimate fate.

The Khrushchev reports intend to do just that. In them the West is challenged to a competitive coexistence across the total frontier of cultural endeavor, with the clear implication that communism is the better of the two systems. However, a challenge is a two-way affair. One is free to declare one's superiority, but when the competition is on there is an open risk that the other side may win.

Ideology remains important and will be invoked for inspiration and propaganda, but in due course practical considerations and results will become determining factors. Ideology will be modified in the light of circumstances. Although scholars are debating the pros and cons of Communist ideology and power, Communist history from Lenin to Khrushchev makes it quite clear that power factors have modified ideology. Even in the reports Marxism-Leninism is used as orthodox Communist doctrine with no suggestion that it either has been modified or will be modified in the course of achieving the declared goals. It is quite obvious that it cannot be publicly acknowledged that the unchanging truth of communism has undergone a change, but the pragmatic use of ideology is quite patent. Khrushchev is invoking Marxist-Leninist stereotypes to justify and institute changes.

There has been developing a gap between Communist theory and practice, ideology and power. Without minimizing the role of ideology, it is becoming clear that in the course of time power considerations will widen the gap between the classical Marxist ideology and current Communist practice. Or we might say that the gap will be so widened by the assimilation of ideology to the power-political demands that it will be hardly recognizable in relation to its original pattern.

In the expansion of communism, nationalism of young and formerly colonial people was used as a means to the realization of

Communist objectives. Many nationalist movements of liberation were subverted and later transformed into Communist movements and governments. It looks as if the strategy and tactics of using nationalism for communism has boomeranged and now nationalism is using communism for its ends.

The strangest thing is that it first happened in the original home of communism, the Soviet Union. That was the crux of the conflict between Stalin and Trotsky. The slogan of "socialism in one country" opened a new chapter in the relationship between nationalism and communism. Prior to that the Soviet Union and Communist world outlook were synonymous. The authority of the Soviet Union and communism were interchangeable. It was one totalitarian whole. Communist parties in the world looked to the Soviet Union for guidance and support, and when policy shift took place in the Kremlin, all Communist parties immediately began to sing the same tune.

In 1948 the consequences of "socialism in one country" became apparent. That was the year that Marshal Tito's Yugoslavia was expelled from the Cominform. Yugoslavia did not repudiate communism. It asserted its right to apply Communist principles and practices in accordance with the genius and needs of Yugoslavia as a nation. Although Soviet and Cominform pressure on Yugoslavia was immense, she was able to ride the storm by dint of her own strength and by timely and understanding help from the West. The claims of nationalism in relationship to communism were vindicated.

There are at the present time many varieties of national communism. Particularly, the Communist parties are being pulled apart by two centers of authority. Moscow and Peking are competing with each other for the allegiance of Communist parties and the headship of the bloc. The rulers of Peking no more use the disguise of Tito to attack Khrushchev's communism, and the masters of the Kremlin do not hide behind Albania to aim their fiery darts at the red dragon of Peking.

It is a fight for power, authority, and the correct interpretation of the dogmas of Marxism-Leninism. The power pursuit of national interests, the variant and heretical interpretations of Communist doctrine, and tendencies toward pluralism not only weaken the totalitarian character of Communist ideology but also enlarge the gap between ideology and power by accentuating the latter.

It could be that just as the secularization of the mission of Russian Orthodox Christendom resulted in Communist messianism, so now through the process of nationalistic pluralism, Communist messianism, having become parochial, has come close to losing its sense of universal mission. Just as Russia never reconciled herself to being just one of the member states of Europe, so also the Soviet Union will find it difficult to be just one of the states in the Communist family of nations. As a matter of historical fact, the question of the destiny of Soviet Russia will haunt her from both directions and with double force. A new version of the Western-Slavophile struggle will rage within the depths of the Soviet Russian soul. Who would provide the channels for the expression of Soviet Russian destiny?

Even if half of the goals and targets set in the Khrushchev reports were realized, the agricultural sufficiency and the industrial productive strength of the Soviet Union would be such that her citizens would begin to enjoy such security, material comfort, and standard of living that mere questions of food, shelter, and clothing would not occupy their attention.

They would demand more intellectual freedom, search for moral values, raise questions about the meaning of life, and even ask religious questions. That man does not live by bread alone but by other things too will become as natural in the Soviet context as in any other context. The Russian humanity burst forth in volcanic creativity of immense quality and quantity when the autocracy and censoriousness of the czars became too much for it to bear. The nineteenth century is a monument to the creative powers of Russian humanity under duress. Russian humanity, because and in spite of Sovietization, has the immense powers of creative manifestation. In science and technology it is making great strides, but who will trigger its flowering in the arts, humanities, and moral and spiritual values?

PRIEST WITHOUT CASSOCK

In the course of discussion, several times the question has come up about the agency which might step into the breach between ideology and power, awaken the sense of destiny in Russian-Soviet humanity, and trigger its humanistic, moral, and spiritual flowering. It is difficult to give an unequivocal answer, but it is reasonable to hope that a regenerated Russian Orthodox Church may be called upon to undertake this most difficult and life-giving task. The church cannot perform this task while wearing the ornate ecclesiastical vestments. It has to take these vestments off and soil its hands in the everyday work of reconstructing humanity.

The church has to act as a "priest without cassock" to mingle with the common stuff of Russian life to wrest from it a form divine. The church has to be secularized and mixed in the world in order to save it. Such a church can only be reckoned with and not beaten. Berdyaev quotes a saying of Lenin to the effect that, "A Roman Catholic priest who seduces a girl is much less dangerous than a 'priest without cassock,' a priest without the crudities of religion, an intelligent and democratic priest who preaches the making of some little god or other, for you can expose the first priest, condemn him and get rid of him, but you cannot get rid of the second so easily, and to expose him is a thousand times more difficult." Lenin meant by the "priest without cassock" anyone who is swayed by idealistic or religious principles and is not a materialist. He is the man who wears the disguise of ideas. There is an element of truth in what Lenin says, but we use the phrase "priest without cassock" to mean that the one who is persuaded by ideas is most concerned with things. The one who teaches the hungry that there is heavenly bread also teaches them that there is material bread, and that man needs both.

In the Russian-Soviet situation of today, the Russian Orthodox Church is called upon to act as a "priest without cassock." There are two possible ways through which the Russian Orthodox Church can come into its own and become an agent of truth and justice for the Russian-Soviet people. The first way is for the church to get deeply and sacrificially involved in the social revolution in Russia. What Christianity failed to do, Marx tried to do; what Marx tried to do has not been done. The question is, can the Russian Orthodox Church do it *now?*

The second way by which the church can recover its initiative and mission is through ecumenism. The Russian Orthodox Church must reach out toward Protestantism and Roman Catholicism, both to help and to be helped, to impart Christian life and strength and to receive them in return. To avail itself of these two ways of self-renewal which in turn become channels of world-renewal, the Russian Orthodox Church will have to use all its long-accumulated wisdom, tact, and prophetic power.

The shadow of Constantine has hung over the Russian Orthodox Church. Russia inherited from Byzantium not only Christianity, but also a particular form of state-church relationship. The emperor reigned supreme over the church, in reverse proportion to Western Christendom where the pope was the lord over kings and princes. The czarist tradition of the omnipotent state was assumed by the Bolsheviks. The Communist totalitarian state is antithetical to the existence of a rival authority within it, particularly if that authority happens to be the church.

As we have already noted, under Stalin a concordat between the state and the church was reached. It is precarious, but it is there. It is a realistic limitation under which the church has to work. As a matter of fact, the church has always lived under such a concordat. Since it has no other experience, it may not know how to change it. Since it has lived with it so long, it may be able to handle it to perform its creative ministry.

The Russian Orthodox Church has to do a lot of housecleaning. It must clearly establish a distinction between religious superstition and honest Orthodox Christianity. It should repudiate the former. The priests should be men of wide culture and impeccable moral character, lovers of humble and ordinary people. The church and its priests should be above reproach so that nobody can expose or condemn them. The Russian Orthodox Church must repent and chasten itself because of its responsibility for the permitting of conditions which led to the formation of communism.

Unless it shares this historic responsibility, it cannot perform the new task.

In Marx's theses on Feuerbach (and in his other writings) he propounded the vision of a new humanity which would be not abstract, but real, concrete, social humanity. This social humanity he envisaged can be brought about by revolutionary practical activity. He wanted to bridge the gap between theory and practice, for he held this gap to be the major defect of philosophy and religion. He did not just want to think about the world; he wanted to change it. He had a messianic purpose concerning the transformation of human society.

Communism has not realized the Marxist vision. The much talked-about new Soviet man and new Soviet civilization are still awaited. All that can be seen is that perhaps an alternative method to achieve economic affluence has arisen, but where is the new Soviet man who is supposed to be quite different from the old Russian man? Communism has created more discipline and organization, but the Russian man with all his native qualities is quite visible through it all.

The Russian Orthodox Church must give priority to the social and ethical sphere, and live and preach—but certainly live more than preach—the social concerns of the Christian faith. The church must show by active participation in the social realities of the Russian-Soviet life that Christian love, truth, and justice have profound stakes in actual existence.

It has been the special contribution of Russian Orthodox thought from Vladimir Soloviev to Nicholas Berdyaev to emphasize the doctrine of God-humanity. This highly original doctrine should not be made a liturgical and doctrinal affair, but more than ever before should be the basis and power of the church's involvement in the processes of personal and social change. The limitations on the church are great, but it must find ways and means to demonstrate that Russian Orthodoxy is that type of social Christianity which wants to live and work where people live and work.

Marxism is a secularization of a part of the Christian truth and reality. And if in the Russian-Soviet situation, the Russian Orthodox Church can help implement the Marxist vision, it will be fulfilling the Christian task. It may also provide the church with an access to Soviet youth, which has so far been denied to it.

Nothing comparable to the nineteenth century has happened in the twentieth; the church can encourage, inspire, and exemplify great literary themes of human pathos, moral courage, intellectual integrity, and religious beauty. It can support the intellectual in setting a new style of intellectual liberation. It is significant to notice that Franz Kafka, whose writings had been banned in the U.S.S.R., has been recently introduced into the Soviet Union.

Two of his stories, "Metamorphosis" and "In the Penal Settlement," were published in one of the numbers of *Foreign Literature,* a popular Soviet magazine. In his native Czechoslovakia, students and teachers have been discussing for some time the relationship of Kafka to existentialism and Marxism. Apparently serious questions are being discussed in Czech intellectual circles. What is surprising is the selection of "In the Penal Settlement" in the Soviet magazine.

"In the Penal Settlement" is a cynical account of the ways of execution in a concentration camp. The victim does not know what he is dying for, but is just killed by a devilish machine which meticulously imprints on the victim's chained body the reason for his excruciating death. Kafka's account was written fifty years ago when the Soviet Union was not even in existence. It is possible that the Soviet intellectuals read between the lines of the writings forebodings of Stalinism and Khrushchevism. The "former commandant" of the colony is dead, but the executioner takes pleasure in telling a foreign visitor that the whole penal colony is his work, and is planned with such perfection that his successor cannot alter a thing. The executioner was the commandant's assistant and knew all about the working of the settlement. The guiding principle is that guilt is never to be doubted. He still uses the plans of the former commandant and they are his prized possession. But under the new, mild doctrine, the resources for maintaining the killing machine have been considerably reduced. The old commandant would suggest the figure of Stalin to the intellectuals, but the story goes on to say that the priest would not permit the body of the old commandant to be buried in the churchyard. Nobody knew for a while where to bury him, but finally they buried him in a house, and the prophecy has it that after a few years the commandant will rise and lead his adherents to capture the colony.

During the post-Stalin period, Soviet intellectuals have taken an increasingly original line to express bold and free thoughts by the device of publishing the writings of great earlier writers. No intelligent Russian reader can miss the symbolic significance of this grim tale. In 1957 Ehrenburg was sharply rebuked for publishing "Lessons of Stendhal," which made the point that what matters is the essence of tyranny rather than the personality of the tyrant. In 1961 Yevtushenko wrote a famous poem which warned against the comeback of the Stalinists. Similarly, Dudintsev and Solzhevytsin have published novels hitting at certain basic concepts of Soviet society. The church must work for the liberalization of intellectual freedom.

The original mission of Russia was embodied in the doctrine of Moscow as the third Rome. This was a religious mission. It was the destiny of Russia to preserve the purity of faith of Russian Orthodox civilization. By the substitution of the godless creed of Marxism-Leninism for Russian Orthodoxy, the religious meaning of destiny was lost. If not lost, it was transformed into a secular messianism. This, as we have seen, has been diluted by nationalist Communist rivalries. Perhaps the Russian Orthodox Church, rejuvenated and possessed of a prophetic power, can restore to the Russian-Soviet people the humane and religious sense of destiny.

The divisions of Christendom are deep and of long standing, but ecumenism can enable the Russian Orthodox Church to get rid of its physical and spiritual isolation. It can be stimulated in thought, word, and deed by Protestantism and Roman Catholicism. This may lead to inner theological productivity which will provide for its clergy rich food for thought, and will also stimulate them to write and think. In return, the other churches will learn from its rich experience of suffering and stamina for survival. Through direct contact, the Western churches will be able to learn and to understand the facts of Russian-Soviet life. Moreover, the bond which participation in ecumenical activity will create will strengthen the church in Russia and lend more power to Christian witness throughout the world.

The Russian Orthodox Church tried to convene an ecumenical

conference of the Orthodox, but did not succeed. She must for her own sake step out from her own enclosed circumstances. Moreover, in the Soviet sphere of influence she will have to deal with Roman Catholics in Poland and Hungary and with Protestants in Czechoslovakia and East Germany. These contacts will be ecumenical and will bring her into touch with people who are deeply influenced by Western Christianity and culture, and are enjoying more freedom. They are relatively free because the Soviet Union cannot afford to have a repetition of the Hungarian revolt or Polish riots.

There is no illusion about the fact that the rulers of the Kremlin will permit the Russian Orthodox Church to act as suggested, but history does not provide opportunities for action at will. Time has to be seized, and possibly this is that time. The concordat is not to be used only for the state but also for the church and the Lord of the church. The crucial question is whether or not the church will rise to the occasion to engage in the task of transfiguring the social life and forms of Russian-Soviet society.

THE SECULARIZATION OF CHRISTIANITY
(*Christianity and Democracy*)

The Reformation is the foundation of the modern liberal democratic state. The liberty of the Christian man and the priesthood of all believers cut the nerve of the absolutism of the pope, king, and state. The Puritan congregation inculcated the spirit of discussion and resolution of conflict by reasoning together under the guidance of the Spirit of God.

The church was a free association of spiritual men under God, and there were other free associations in society for the growth and advancement of the individual. The state was also such an association. Society was larger than the state. Everything in society was under the supervening grace of God, and even when separation of church and state took place, the ethics of the church inspired the whole society. From the very beginning of the democratic state to the present, there has been a persistent conviction of its deep relationship to Protestant Christianity. Even the French Politiques did not deny a place to religion when they were, in preference to religion, focusing their attention on the centralizing power of nationality. The latest evidence of the persistent and abiding relationship of democracy to Christianity in particular and to religion in general is found in the concluding remarks of the report to the President entitled "Goals for Americans." The report asserts that the American democratic society is a spiritually based society.

On the other hand, as we have observed in Chapter IV, there has been a progressive secularization of Protestant Christianity in the development of political, liberal democracy. The French Revolution above all made democracy a universal outlook which could be exported to the rest of the world and could compete with other viewpoints, the Christian viewpoint not excepted. From its inception in the Reformation, through English and American Puritanism, the American experiment and Revolution, the French Revolution, and British utilitarianism to American pragmatism, liberal democracy has gathered such momentum and integrated so many diverse elements that it has become a competitive world outlook. It has become the de facto religion of the Western man, displacing Christianity from its focal position and deeply secularizing it.

The Wars of Religion displaced Christianity in favor of the political principle, emphasizing that if Christianity cannot be the rallying point, but turns out to be destructive of the process of Western civilization, then nationality may be the gravitating center which can save the nation as well as Western civilization.

The British utilitarians, faced with the phenomenon of rising industrialism, emphasized the efficient state and free trade by open competition. Being believers in the law of contract and the harmony of interests, they taught that free pursuit of individual interest guided by contract will lead to the harmony of the interests of all. Modern technological achievements and complexities of economic and political life have reinforced the utilitarians' point of the efficient and powerful state. The individual pursues his interest in a ruthless mechanical way as part of a great corporate organization, ending up, as a result, somewhat less than an individual.

It appears from the course of history since the Wars of Religion that Christianity has progressively taken a receding position in relation first to the political, then to the economic, and last but certainly not least, to the individual self-interest principle. The connection between Christianity and liberal democracy has not been severed, but first place belongs to the individual self and to the state, to the pursuit of what is called enlightened self-interest and the practice of patriotism. In one sense, the emphasis on the individual has done a lot of disservice to Christianity. The stress on the individual has emphasized that religion is a private affair.

This has given rise to a habit of thought which eclipses the social significance and function of Christianity. It is indeed important for the individual to think for himself, and there is a privacy of the self which is inviolable, but it does not follow from this that what one believes and thinks does not affect others. The privacy of religious belief has created such a pervasive habit of thought that sincere and honest people are horrified to learn that Christian belief should be actively involved in community affairs and the process of social change.

In a competitive society there is always the possibility and the fact that the pursuit of economic and other self-interests, even though regulated by law and contract, will transgress the moral and spiritual sensitivities. The conflict between the legal and moral and the disparity between business ethics and Christian ethics are not occasional occurrences of our business civilization. Moreover, the pursuit of economic self-interest is so high-pressured that it reduces Christianity to a Sunday religion and tends to lead to mental and physical sickness and exhaustion. Yet the frantic pursuit goes on as if a devotee is following his god. People hot on the pursuit of self-interest tend to increase in selfishness and decrease in the sense of community. Perhaps this is the result of having lost original moorings in the Christian ethos.

When the Industrial Revolution began to affect the life of Western society practically, the state and government as originally thought by the Puritans could not cope with the complexity of economic, political, and social problems. The state acquired more power and organizational complexity that, rather than being an organization of society, became the most powerful organization in society. And under the technological impact of the modern age it has become so powerful that sometimes it is difficult to distinguish between society and the state.

Certainly in relation to the church, the power, authority, and omnicompetence of the state have no comparison. Originally the state was limited in favor of the church; now the church is circumscribed in favor of the state. Because of the pre-eminent position of the state, patriotism enjoys pre-eminence also. The democratic state is not a totalitarian state; however, its relative position and strength in relation to other free associations of society are so preponderant that its admiration is easy and popular, but its defiance is difficult and consequential. But in the name of God and conscience it can be defied, and this separates it qualitatively from a totalitarian state.

Faced with the overwhelming power of the modern democratic state, people take refuge in the past and advocate return to federalism and states' rights, or invoke the model of the Puritan congregation. These people want to close their eyes to the urgencies and complexities of the present national and world situation and to return to some fancied past which was never there. These are anachronisms, found in the churches and in society at large. They may serve as warnings, but they are no solutions to the problems at hand. The strength of the state is clearly out of proportion to the strength of the church, but the separation of church and state is intact and there is no visible danger of either Caesaropapism or Papocaesarism.

SOCIAL REVOLUTION IN AMERICA

Christianity has been displaced in practice if not in lip service by liberal democracy, and Christian obedience has been superceded by patriotism and the pursuit of self-interest. There is no outright repudiation of Christianity. The churches are well attended on Sunday. It could be that a lot of people hold a variety of attitudes which are mixtures of Christianity, democracy, patriotism, and enlightened or unenlightened self-interest. The separation of church and state makes for a working compatibility between Christianity and democracy. Christian people are apt to suffer from the majority illusion.

The Christian church is a minority, and the sooner it realizes this the better it will be for its future and for the future of the nation. The Christian minority is not ethnic; it is the minority of Christian belief, commitment, and practice. It should come alive and perform its role as a prophetic and creative minority. It should act as a leaven in the dough, the salt of the earth, the light unto the nations, and the saving remnant of God. It must repent for not living the Christian life and for permitting the treasures of God entrusted to it to be changed into an alien substance.

The only way the Christian church in America can regain its original vision and mission is to give a living and practical demonstration of what it believes in and lives by. It is not the social gospel which the church should preach; it is the love, justice, and truth of Christ that the church must live today, for tomorrow may be too late.

The urgencies and the needs of the social situation of humanity are such that the church must participate in them. The ongoing social revolution in America provides the church with a historic opportunity to redeem itself by redeeming the personal and social condition of American humanity.

The Negro is the displaced person of American humanity. He has made his church his home. He lives in it and lives by it. He prays to gain strength, sings to give thanks, and lays at the altar of the Lord his life, so that he may receive life, liberty, and happiness. His ministers stay with him shoulder to shoulder. From the house of the Lord which has made them feel at home, the Negroes march into the inhospitable world of man. Beaten and bruised but never discouraged, they return home to be replenished in order to march again. Every march is not a mere repetition; the same distance is not gone over again. Every time there is some kind of gain. The Negro "diaspora" kindles the flame of love, justice, and fellowship in the church on the other side of the great divide. They come from the north, the south, the east, and the west; the procession of freedom becomes so immense that spectators become marchers, and as they march side by side they look at each other and are strengthened by the bond of common faith.

Democracy has Christian sources, and there is a Christian

conscience hidden somewhere in democracy. When the Supreme Court of the United States ruled in favor of desegregation to the pleadings of Thurgood Marshall, it was the manifestation of the Christian conscience through the democratic process. The passing of the Civil Rights Bill by the legislature through the active guidance and support of the executive branch is not merely a political but a moral act. This is also a manifestation of the Christian heritage through the democratic process. However, there is still a long road ahead.

The wholehearted participation of the church, which has not yet come about in the American social revolution, will perform two eminent tasks and achieve two equally eminent results. The successful outcome of the social revolution will consummate the goal of nation building, something for which American history has been striving. Secondly, the social revolution may be completed by the Negro's achievement of equality with his fellow Americans, but these two sections of American humanity may still remain spiritually strangers to each other. Here the redemptive and reconciling ministry of the church should lend every resource it possesses in the service of uniting the spirit of one man to the spirit of another man.

If the American social revolution is consummated in this manner, there is nothing that the American people have to fear from the Communists or from any other quarter. The nations of Asia, Africa, and Latin America will see the truth and will not have to be convinced. What has been said sounds like a dream, but at the juncture of history where we stand it is not an unreasonable dream.

Along with participation in the American social revolution, the church must reinforce its ecumenical activities. To have life is to have it with others. There will be abundant Christian life when constructive and fruitful channels have been formed among the Protestant, Roman Catholic, and Orthodox sections of the Body of Christ. The more united the ecumenical church becomes, the more effective will her witness be to the world in which she lives. Only in this way will the people of the world know that those who are in the church and participate in the world are the people of God and his Christ.